☐The Wisdomkeepers☐

Tehachapi Women of Substance

↪ Judith Campanaro ↩

The Wisdom Keepers
Tehachapi Women of Substance
by Judith Campanaro

Copyright © 2019, Judith Campanaro

Editing: Jane Zeok
Cover: photo Purina Paparotti Polillo
          The author's grandmother - her personal wise woman

To Susanna —
My hero,
you are absolutely
special and
wonderful.
Love, Judith

DEDICATION

For Jane Zeok, Andi Hicks, and Joseph Rooney

Thank you for all your help, support, and encouragement.
Bless you for being you and for sharing your wisdom and
inspiration.

CONTENTS

Sherrie Ann Beaty Harris - She Traveled the World

Betty Flores - A Woman of Strength

Lauraine Snelling - An Extraordinary Gift

Afterword:

The Forgotten Talent

Will You Come Out and Play

I'm Just Looking for Something

Do You Want to Know What's Wrong

ACKNOWLEDGEMENTS

First and foremost, I want to thank my brilliant editor, Jane Zeok. You were so encouraging throughout the entire process of writing. You were receptive to my thoughts and have helped me to reformat them and make them better. I am so appreciative.

I express gratitude to all of the wonderful women of Tehachapi who allowed me to interview them and share their stories. I learned so much from each of you.

Thank you Tina Unthank for your thoughtfulness and for always being there when I needed a friend the most.

Thank you Kristina Herrera for your photographs and inspiration. Thank you Andi and Neil Hicks for your help with all things technical, from filming video to operating the silhouette machine. You've been a great help.

And most of all, I am thankful for all of my friends who supported me in this venture.

FORWARD

I don't know why I started writing this book. It's just something I felt I had to do. Oftentimes during the process, I asked myself why I even continued with a project that seemed, at times, so daunting. But I kept going and I'm glad I did. I hope you, the reader, will be glad as well. It is my hope that you will also find the treasures within that have provided me with guidance in the journey of life.

Walking the Senior path, is not an easy adventure. There are so many unknowns and new vistas to explore. In my own life, I've wondered some days, "Who am I? Why am I still here? Does what I do really matter?" There were times when I've felt invisible, when I've been forced to acknowledge change in both my physical and cognitive abilities. No one wanted to hear my opinion, or so I thought. There were aches and pains that slowed me down;. and I can't forget the loss of youth.

The repercussions of that loss often foster symptoms of PTSD. No, becoming a senior is not easy, and yet there is hope. The "third age" can be accompanied by not only new vision and reinvention of the self, but also most importantly, acceptance; acceptance of what has been, what is now, and what is to come.

It has taken me a long time to accept each change as a gift in a new disguise, and to see the depth of wisdom earned with countless life experiences.

Renowned developmental psychologist, Eric Erikson, teaches us that during each stage of life a person experiences a psychosocial crisis which could have a positive or negative outcome. Ego integrity versus despair is the eighth and final stage of Erik Erikson's theory. This stage begins at approximately age 65 and ends at death. During the stage of integrity versus despair, people reflect back on the life they have lived and come away with either a sense of fulfillment from a life well-lived or a sense of regret and despair over a life misspent. This can be a time to reapply, adapt, and transfer wisdom to new areas of life. By drawing upon the skills and knowledge gained, life can be reinvented and our vision of what has been can be reframed.

And maybe that's why I wrote this book, to reframe lives well-lived. I didn't want to interview our "local historians" whose voices have been heard and published many times. No, I wanted to highlight the personal and unspoken nature of my neighbors and friends.

As I asked women if I could interview them, more often than not the answer was, "Why would you want to interview me? I just have an ordinary life with nothing much to share." But that was exactly what I was looking for.

I wanted to tell the stories of women who have lived "ordinary" lives in extraordinary ways. Because everyone, whether they believe it or not, has something wonderful to offer. We each come with our own gifts and talents, and more often than not, we diminish the value of our contributions.

Acceptance is about letting go of the idea that you must be something other than what you are. Imagine looking at yourself right now and seeing everything you are, not everything you are not. Imagine living life not from a place of discontent, but from a place of self-worth and satisfaction. And imagine taking a moment to simply acknowledge the fact that *I am what I am and I am who I am, and that is okay.*

In this book, I share with you the stories of women whose voices have gone unheard. Stories have a way of helping us connect with parts of ourselves. How we react and relate to the narratives of others can lead us to a profound reflection of our own personal life experiences.

In a recent blog, Tamara La Porte, founder of willowing.org, captured this concept so well:

> *"I've noticed for myself that stories like fairy tales, myths and even current fiction or other people's 'real life' stories, help me go deeper within myself and help me capture forgotten or lost feelings and experiences. At times, it also helps me face my demons and look at things I've been too afraid to look at. The more I sit with the stories and ask myself how the events relate to my own life, the more I deepen my understanding of and connection with myself and the world around me. The metaphors and symbolism in the old stories offer such rich ways to explore the meaning of life and our own existence. Like with many other art forms, stories open*

doorways into the felt experiences that help us grow, remember, transform and learn more about ourselves."

Storytelling is an important human tradition. There are many scriptures from all religions and cultures that reflect on the essential value of narrative. The stories of our lives teach us to love, to forgive others, to be just, and to strive for a better existence.

The Life Story Commons was established in 1988. Their mission has been to celebrate individual lives and strengthen community bonds by bringing people of all generations together to share life stories. According to the Commons,

"Life storytelling is a kind of spiritual endeavor in which we get to the heart of who we are and what is most important to us. Our own life stories can be tools for making us whole; they gather up the parts of us and put them together in a way that gives our lives greater meaning than they had before we told our story. The stories we tell of our own lives carry this transforming power, too. Our stories illustrate our inherent connectedness with others. In the life story, each person is a reflection of another's life story. In some mysterious, amazing way our stories and our lives are all tied together."

And so, I present to you my gift, *""Wisdom Keepers, Tehachapi Women of Substance."* It is my hope that these little vignettes of remarkable people traveling life as teachers, artists, and homemakers will, in some small way, encapsulate for you the quiet grandeur of living everyday lives with beauty, grace, power, and flair. May these women inspire you into victorious, ascendant aging, with feelings of self-satisfaction, release, fulfillment and completion.

Softly,
Judith Campanaro

"Open to me, so that I may open.
Provide me your inspiration so that I might see mine."
-RUMI

PREFACE

Over the past several years I have developed a strong curiosity about the aging process. I readily concede that this interest is most likely due to my own aging. Nevertheless, as a result, I embarked on a study of the third age. Often defined as the span of time between retirement and the beginning of age-imposed limitations, beginning around the age of 65.

Several years ago, while on vacation in Halifax, my dear friends, John Perry and Brenda Hoddinot, introduced me to wonderful stories and books about aging. I spent my two week retreat in Canada devouring those books.

At one point, John asked me why I was so concerned about dying? I tried to explain it wasn't my fear of death that peaked my interest, but rather curiosity about how others navigated this journey. Seeing how active elders overcame struggles and difficulties in their lives and maintained a sense of integrity intrigued me. I wanted to know more.

After returning home, I started interviewing friends and neighbors in my home town of Tehachapi, California. Each of the stories they told brought prominent themes to the table: continuity, commitment, purpose, family. Seeking to find relevance in the narratives, I began to wonder if the person being interviewed recognized the overall significance of their life.

That is why before each interview I added a commentary about how each individual had touched my life, how knowing them had added to my personal history and journey. To me, each person I interviewed became a gift, someone I heard and who was hearing me. The interviews were not extensive, only highlights of lives well lived filled with nuggets of wisdom to be mined and digested. These stories are very likely ones that others share. They teach us something about life, validating our own experience while pointing out that we are never alone. The more we share our own stories the closer we all become.

To add further meaning and personal enrichment, after each interview I have added an exercise for your own deeper self-discovery. As an art therapist and empowerment coach, my mission has always been to facilitate empowerment through creative expression. You don't have to be 65 or older to enjoy this book. Regardless of your age, my hope is that these stories and exercises will serve as a source of inspiration and become additional resources to help you navigate whatever life throws your way.

CHAPTER 1
"THE CRUISING QUEEN"
LUPE BARAJAS

Whenever I visit Lupe Barajas she greets me with graciousness and open arms. And when I leave she always thanks me for coming. I assure her the visit benefits me more than her. I explain that she is an inspiration and almost like a mentor in this elder hood journey. Several years ago Lupe developed macular degeneration. I asked her how she deals with the loss of her sight. Lupe responded that, "I just go one day at a time. Attitude is everything". Her answer reminded me of a friend I met several years ago who also suffered a loss. I asked if she minded not having any legs. My friend's response was to quote something she read in The Reader's Digest years ago: *"The only disability is a bad attitude."*

Lupe's positive attitude is a gift. I have learned so many things from her. She reminds me that the important thing is to enjoy everything you do the moment you do it. And if something is not done effortlessly, then forget it. Lupe reminds me not to put faith in things that are not necessary to put faith in. "If it has to happen, it will happen anyway," she says. I give thanks for this beautiful woman. And thanks to Lupe I am watching my attitude in all that I do.

"If you don't like something, change it.
If you can't change it, change your attitude."
Maya Angelo

LUPE BARAJAS

She's elegance personified. This lovely woman radiates heartfelt wisdom and a timeless love for others. Lupe Barajas was born in Colorado, the youngest of fifteen children. Life often brought tragedy and only six of the fifteen children survived. When Lupe was eleven years old, her mom died. Lupe's dad moved the remaining family to California where his sisters helped raise the children.

While living with her aunt, Lupe excelled in school and developed a strong work ethic. Because her parents had come from Mexico, she was fluent in both Spanish and English. She loved to read and won lots of spelling bees. Lupe's dad was a professional card player and she inherited his skills with math and critical thinking. As she grew older, Lupe volunteered at her elementary school where she tutored fourth graders in spelling. Says Lupe, "I had a simple life with lots of joy. My two brothers and three sisters are all deceased now but we had a wonderful time when we were together." Her joy is still with her today and obvious to anyone who spends time with Lupe.

At the age of eighteen Lupe and her older sister moved out on their own. Lupe worked in a tamale factory. One of her work associates introduced her to Julian Barajas. It was love at first sight and they met in February 1958 and were married in July 1958. Lupe said, "When I was single I always lived with others. I never had a home just for me. Julian didn't want me to work after our marriage so I became a homemaker. I liked decorating the house and making a home. And I was a good cook. I always made Julian's favorite beans with chili and homemade tortillas." Julian worked at the "Wham-O" toy factory, and because Lupe liked to paint and color she used her skills to work at home assembling and painting toys.

Julian and Lupe made their home in El Monte, California. The Barajas had lots of friends in the community. They liked to travel and loved road trips. Lupe remembers visiting San Francisco, Sacramento and especially the Southwest. In 1985, a friend gave Lupe the nickname "the cruising queen". The name has stuck ever since. "Every Sunday afternoon," said Lupe, "We would get in the car, buy soda and chips and go wherever the wind blew."

In their second year of marriage Lupe and Julian had a baby girl, Rebecca. When "Becky" was 14 they adopted Anthony. Anthony's parents lived in Mexico, and they already had twelve children when Anthony was born. They felt they simply couldn't afford to keep him. They had met Lupe and Julian through friends and were thankful for the help from the Barajas family and their willingness to adopt their son Anthony. Lupe graciously welcomed Anthony into their home. As Anthony grew Lupe and Julian became very active in little league baseball. They served on the Board of Directors for ten years. Anthony was a great "little leaguer" and Becky excelled in school. Lupe knew she had done her job well. Then when Becky was a senior in high school Lupe decided to enroll in CNA training. She worked as a caregiver until both she and Julian retired at the age of 59.

Becky got married on her parent's 37th wedding anniversary. After the ceremony Lupe and Julian renewed their own vows. It was truly a memorable day and brought a close family even closer. Lupe and Julian retired shortly after this, and moved in with Becky and her husband who lived in

Tehachapi. They now have nine grandchildren, seven from Anthony and two from Becky.

Looking back on her life, Lupe's advice is to treat others with respect but above all to respect your self. "And before you leave the house in the morning, make sure your bed is made and the dishes are done," she continued. "If you make your bed every morning you will have accomplished the first task of the day and it will remind you that the little things in life matter."

ATTITUDE IS EVERYTHING

The Greek Stoic philosopher, Epictetus, taught us that men are disturbed not by things, but by the view which they take of them. It is often our thoughts that create the majority of stress in our lives. Changing stressful thoughts changes one's outlook and releases tension.

Albert Ellis, the founder of Rational Emotive Therapy, also teaches us that perception and thought create one's reality. The key is you have a choice. Any issue can be reframed. Consider the yin-yang symbol. Everything has a positive and negative side. Choose the positive affirmations you really want to hear. The greatest magic carpet is your imagination. You are in harmony if your basic attitude lets you live in peace. By using your thoughts and creative self to bring about peace and contentment, your energy level will increase.

SIMPLE TIME OUT EXERCISE

Sit quietly in a comfortable space where you won't be disturbed. Think of the phrase "ah ha," you know, that "ah ha!" moment when you really get it? While you are thinking of the phrase, stop for a moment after the "ah." Stay in the space between the "ah" and the "ha." Remain in the quietude for as long as you can.

·   Were you able to stay in that space without thoughts intruding?
·   Was it hard to be still?

Doing this exercise even for one minute will prove to be helpful in learning to hear your still small voice. Don't worry. The more you do it, the easier it gets. And don't be surprised if you attitude improves!

CHAPTER 2
SHE SOWED A GARDEN OF BEAUTIFUL DEEDS
CARMEN CAPETILLO

"Old age offers the opportunity to shift from our cares away from the physical toward what cannot be taken away-
our wisdom and the love we offer those around us."
-Ram Dass

Carmen's English is limited and so is my Spanish so I interviewed her granddaughter Angela for Carmen's story. Hearing about her life totally made sense because one thing I can say about Carmen is that she exudes pure love. When Carmen greets you it is with the biggest smile you've ever seen. Her smile warms and touches the heart. I love to visit Carmen because I always come away with a sense of spiritual presence. She reminds me that as we age we learn to see through new eyes. Sometimes when we visit I just sit and massage her hands. Her graciousness and spirit need no words or explanation. When Carmen looks at me with her eyes and her smile I am always reminded that unconditional love is everything. We don't have to talk. Carmen's probably thankful for that because my Spanish is horrible!

CARMEN CAPETILLO

Carmen Capetillo was born in Monolith, California in 1925. Her father worked in the cement plant and Carmen was born in the village just outside of the plant where the employees lived. Carmen and her four siblings lived a happy, simple life until one day when her father left. Without a father to support everyone, Carmen's mother moved the family to Mexico.

When she was 13, and considered old enough to work, Carmen's aunt who lived in El Paso Texas brought Carmen to the United States. Carmen got a job in a sewing factory. Always a giver, she sent the money she made to her mother to help raise her siblings. When her brother was old enough to work, he got a job and took over the family responsibility.

It was in her travels between visiting family in Mexico and working in El Paso that Carmen met her husband. They started a family and had four boys together. A few years later, sponsored by a cousin who worked at the cement factory, they moved to Tehachapi. Carmen was finally home once again.

A stay at home mom, Carmen took her job to heart. Every morning she arose at 4am to make fresh tortillas. She cooked, cleaned, took care of her boys and her husband and loved being a wife and mom. Carmen fought hard for her kids. She fought for them to finish school when her husband said they needed to quit and go to work. When the boys were in junior high they wanted clothes from the store. They didn't want hand me downs or the ones Carmen made. Not having money to buy new clothes, Carmen got a job as a dishwasher at Kelsey's. Not only did the boys get their new "duds" but

Carmen learned English. She credits the staff at Kelsey's for teaching her and giving her a new skill.

All of her boys played sports. They grew up to be fine young men but not without hardship for Carmen. Her son Armando died in a car accident and her father died a year later on the same day. Rudy grew up to be a career military man. He has three boys and one grandchild. Victor retired and now umpires baseball. He also has three children and one grandchild. Javier manages a restaurant and catering business. He has three children and four grandchildren.

One day a young man knocked on Carmen's door. He said he was her brother. Carmen's father had started another family in Mexico. The brother looked for and found Carmen and they became close friends. He became a part of her already large family.

In the year 2000, after 55 years of marriage, Carmen's husband said he was moving back to Mexico. Carmen had a hard working life with her "macho man". She told him to go but she was not going with him. She stayed married and let him leave.

Carmen stayed in Tehachapi after her husband left. She kept the home fires burning on her own.

She was a strong woman and always gave of herself. She helped at her local church kitchen and whenever she could she sat with families to give caregivers a rest. Carmen created a network of friends who checked on each other and took care of one another. She made baby sweaters for anyone who had a baby and never charged for them. She said that was her gift. She cooked and took food to those in need and constantly sowed a legacy of good deeds and love. Carmen liked everybody and everybody liked Carmen. She was proud of her garden and yard and she shared the fruits of her labor with everyone. She was a testimony to homemaking. That was Carmen's life and that is what she did.

Now in her 90's she still has a smile that lights up the room and warms your heart. Carmen's message to others is "take time for your loved ones, you never know what the future holds."

AN EXERCISE IN LOVING YOURSELF

In a recent interview with Ernest Chu, author of *Soul Currency,* he asked the question "what would you do if one of your friends started repeating to everyone around you the things you say about yourself?" You'd probably get angry and say who's spreading all these lies and rumors.
WHAT DO YOU SAY?

In your journal:
• Make a list of the things you say about yourself.
• Would you be angry if other people said those things about you?
• Ask your friends if they think the things you say are true?
• Can you think of a time when the words you used made a difference?

Write a Letter to Yourself
The exercise of writing a letter will help you practice forgiving yourself. This tool will begin healing your feelings of regret.

1. Decorate your envelope and the front of your notecard using colored pencils or markers

2. Write a letter to yourself on the inside of your notecard. Talk to yourself as you might talk to a close friend.

3. Remind yourself that you deserve the best in life even if you made mistakes, because you are human and all humans make mistakes.

4. Mail the letter to yourself.

Write in Your Journal
• Write about three objects that are important to you.
• List some difficult losses you have faced.
• Have you ever pretended that a loss was not painful?
• Write about being hopeful. What does this mean to you?
• Write about what makes your heart sing.
• Write about the last time your heart wore a smile.

CHAPTER 3
A WOMAN WITH A PURPOSE
MOLLY SHERMAN

"I've been busy - too busy. It's time to hear from the one that lives in our body."
Ram Dass

Speaking with Molly Sherman reminded me of the importance of presence. Molly views things from a soul perspective and her wisdom is infectious. She doesn't need a lot of words to explain herself. It's simple. She just is who she is and that's enough. What we do in the world is our spiritual practice and the way we give back. Spiritual growth pulled Molly out of depression when she listened to her inner wisdom and learned massage. To this day, Molly shares her gift of healing with others through massage, music and community involvement. Her story reminds me of the importance of self-care and slowing down. Busyness can be a thief that robs us of some of the most fruitful experiences of life. Molly makes her wisdom felt just by her calm demeanor.

MOLLY SHERMAN

Born and raised in Coalinga, California, Molly Sherman moved to Tehachapi in 1967 and has resided here ever since. She studied massage therapy at the Institute of Holistic Studies in 1988 and opened her massage practice in 1989.

Molly grew up with a natural health background. She said, "Back then everything was organic. That's the way things were grown. My mother taught us about helpful remedies and about foot reflexology." Many years later Molly started doing reflexology on friends and family. Her intention was to take a course and do that as a business but life had different plans. An event in 1984 caused her to suffer severe depression. After reading an article in a woman's magazine that recommended massage as an aid for depression Molly got a massage. She said the treatment made her feel so much better that she decided to pursue massage therapy instead of reflexology. When her husband passed away in 1988 Molly did just that and has been practicing ever since.

She says, "When I got that massage, I was in depression and it helped me so much physically and mentally that I decided that's what I wanted to do. There is so much pain out there, both mental and physical, and I wanted to help relieve that pain. That's what started me. I felt massage was so helpful I wanted to offer that gift."

Sherman doesn't have a name for the kind of massage she does. She says over the years she has learned deep tissue work and how to feel in the moment what a person needs. Basically she sticks to a Swedish routine but does the massage a lot differently manipulating muscles. One customer said, "I've had none other like it. It's a Molly massage."

When she first started out Molly said she was new and unsure and found that she was too tense as she worked. She began to teach herself to relax as she was working and says that technique taught her to be relaxed in life. She realized a long time ago that by releasing and relaxing, her body would become like a sieve and the pain would not stick but just go right through. Her advice about life is to lighten up. Molly said "all of our spiritual masters and teachers teach us to lighten up. We take life too seriously. A merry heart does good like medicine as the scripture says."

When she's not doing massage, Molly likes to read and play the piano. She also sings with the Tehachapi Symphonic Chorus. Her two children both currently reside in Tehachapi. She has four grandchildren, two in Oregon, one who recently graduated with a masters from Irvine and a grandson with a BA from Fresno State.

When asked about wisdom she has gleaned over the years Molly says, "Just let it go, relax and go within. Everything we have and need to know is inside of us but sometimes we need guidance along the way. It's about looking in and being more accepting and understanding of yourself. You don't have to go out and make things happen. Just observe."

Her words are well said. Thank you Molly Sherman, for helping others to "lighten up!" and for sharing your gifts with Tehachapi.

IMPRESS YOURSELF EXERCISE

A student in one of my children's art classes said "I like art because I impress myself!" That statement made me chuckle but it also made me think. How many times do you impress yourself? Here's a challenge for you. For the next week or so primp your body. And by primp I mean take special time for grooming, exercise and feel good "stuff". Treat yourself like you are that special someone. Whether you know it or not, believe it or not, you are that special someone. There is no one else exactly like you.

Here are some recipes for massage oils:

Oil with herbs:

½ cup oil (olive, almond or jojoba are my favorites)

1 tbsp fresh herbs of combination of herbs

I like to use fresh herbs because of their strong scent. Rosemary is good for energy, stamina and memory. Oregano boosts circulation. Mint increases metabolism.

Chamomile relaxes and helps create a restful sleep. Lavender soothes, calms and helps with headaches. Basil is good for stress and concentration.

Mix the oil and herbs together. Microwave on high for 2 minutes. Cool the mixture for about 30 minutes. Filter out the solids by pouring through a coffee filter into a bottle. Save an extra sprig or two and place inside the mixture.

Sore Muscles:

Camphor has a soothing and cooling effect on the skin. Eucalyptus oil also works as a muscle soother. You can find both at the drug store or purchase them as essential oils. Add

½ teaspoon of camphor or eucalyptus (just a few drops if you use the essential oils) to ½ cup of your favorite carrier oil.

Citrus Oil

Any combination of citrus zest creates an uplifting oil. Citrus oils are invigorating, uplifting and they have antidepressant qualities. They also help to neutralize acid in the body and stimulate the immune system to fight infections.

½ cup assorted citrus zest

½ cup carrier oil

Place the zest in a glass bowl and pour the oil over it. Heat in the microwave for about two minutes. Cool completely. Remove the zest with a slotted spoon or coffee filter and pour the oil into a bottle.

And now for the fun part - give yourself a massage.

Using your favorite oil mixture take at least thirty minutes to massage yourself. Start with your feet and gradually work up to your scalp. Discover and massage every inch of your body that you can reach. Send loving thoughts to yourself as you begin to release and relax.

CHAPTER 4
A SMILE THAT WARMS THE HEART
KAREN STEVENS

Whenever I think of Karen I feel like a warm hug. She is absolutely delightful. Karen's sense of joy is contagious. I always smile when I'm around her listening to her share her wisdom and adventures. In her book Crones Don't Whine, Jean Bolan tells us "A crone is a woman who has wisdom, compassion, humor, courage and vitality." Karen is all that and more. A woman with zest, passion and soul Karen is a true gift. Just being in her presence constantly reminds me of the importance of joy and of delighting in the gift of being alive. It's an inner happiness that connects us to the moment. Thank you Karen for reminding me to laugh and be grateful. You are the best!

"Dance with your consciousness wherever it might flow."
-Ram Dass

KAREN STEVENS

"I like things to happen, and if they don't happen I like to make them happen."
Winston Churchill

If you want to get the job done just ask Karen Stevens. She has a special ability to cut through the confusion and dodge any head-on collisions. Karen takes all the reasons something can't be done and replaces them with better ways to accomplish it.

A California girl, Karen was born in Santa Monica. Her dad was in the service and when he retired, the family moved to Arvin where Karen grew up and finished school. Karen married her first husband in 1962. The couple moved to Bakersfield in the early 70s to start a swimming pool business. Unfortunately the business went under and so did the marriage. Karen moved to Fresno, worked as a bookkeeper, met a wonderful man, and married him. They were together for 17 years. Eventually they moved back to Bakersfield to help Karen's elderly parents. After her father died, her mother came to live with them. Six months after her mother died, Karen's husband passed away. It takes a strong woman to keep going after so much grief. But keep going she did.

When Karen was in high school she had dated a young boy named Bill. She knew him all through school and they had great times together. According to Karen, Bill was a "jock", drove a fast car, and his mother owned a restaurant that had a "pool table". Karen's dad didn't approve and told Bill not to come around his daughter. But true love always finds a way. She was reacquainted with Bill through a mutual friend. They were married six months later.

Both of them were widowed. Bill had been married for 30 years. He and his wife had dreamed of living in the mountains but they couldn't afford it. Karen's husband had also loved the mountains, the abundant wildlife, taking long walks,and he had wanted to live in a place like that. Karen and Bill not only had the commonality of grade school years in Arvin, but felt they also had the commonality of the shared dreams of the people they had each loved. In 2006, they moved to Tehachapi. Karen said, "It was the combination of similar backgrounds,culminating with getting to actualize together, the dreams of those we had dearly loved."

Karen said when she was growing up in Arvin she had an uncle who lived in Tehachapi. One of her favorite childhood memories was visiting her uncle and picking cherries. She had always wanted to live here. Karen and Bill bought a cabin in Bear Valley. Bill remodeled the house from a weekend cabin to a beautiful home. As the couple got older they realized it was too far out, and made a decision to sell. Knowing that they are of an age where they have to be concerned that one of them might be left alone, they bought a place where either one could afford the payment on their own. Bill is now busy remodeling their new home.

Karen is busy at the Treasure Trove. Karen said, "My grandmother had a wooden rocker with a drawer of yarn and needles inside. I would sit beside her, and she taught me to knit and crochet. I like being creative and especially love teaching fiber arts. I now have a little store at the Treasure Trove. I'm having a ball. It gives me something to do, and gets me out of the house. Teaching feeds me inside and I like guiding customers on their projects. I feel like I'm doing a service."

Recently Karen became one of the partners at the Treasure Trove. Says Karen, "I was thrilled when I was invited to be a partner and feel it is a privilege. My early career was a bookkeeper and I'm really excited to get back to what I loved. I hope to be here for a long while. The people here are family and that's the feel I get in the store, with all the teachers, the students, the volunteers. It's just one great big family."

Karen's advice to others is to like yourself because no one else will if you don't. And to follow the golden rule which is to treat others the way you want to be treated. If you like yourself it is easy to like others, because then you can accept others even if they are different from you.

THE GRATITUDE DANCE

Several years ago I had the opportunity to interview Louise Hay, author of "You Can Heal Your Life" and owner of Hay House Productions. When asked if there was one thing to tell people to do that would help them on their journey, what would it be? Louise answered, "Look in the mirror and say, I love you, I really, really love you. It is the most powerful statement we can make and when we look in our own eyes and do it we connect with that inner child. What the inner child in us really wants is to be loved and feel safe. When you do that it's like miracles happen in your life and all the pieces fall in place. Just enjoy life. Life is meant to be fun. Keep that in mind. You are wonderful and you deserve only the best. Life loves you. And the other thing I would suggest that you do is go to www.juniorattractors.com. They have a gratitude dance. Do it every morning of your life!"

CHAPTER 5
LIVING OUT LOUD!
JUANITA NEIMEYER

"Art should be something like a good armchair
in which to rest from physical fatigue."
Henri Matisse

The beauty and concept of art surrounds us on a daily basis. Mother Earth, the greatest artist of all, fills our hearts and souls with her mountains, forests, lakes, and sunsets.. In his book, Flow, Mihaly Csikszentihalyi teaches us that the very nature of the creative act invokes and induces inner harmony. There is solace in creative endeavors. The end result is not important. It is the process that becomes the healing balm. Juanita Neimeyer has dedicated her life to helping others experience the healing power of art through her gifts of teaching, writing, and painting.

The world is full of wonders that we often don't see until some part of our brain and soul is reawakened. The act of creating brings you moments when you drop your cares and feed that part of you that needs nourishment from the beauty of the world around you. Thank you Juanita for sharing your gift with all of us.

JUANITA NEIMEYER

The French Novelist, Emile Zola was known as a defender of truth and justice Zola said, "If you ask me what I came to do in this world, I, an artist, will answer you: I am here to live out loud." Artist, Juanita Neimeyer is the embodiment of "living out loud."

Born in Kansas, at an early age, she discovered art as her path in life. When she was in the second grade her teacher contacted Niemeyer's parents and asked if Juanita could join her art class. Juanita took private art lessons from the second grade all through high school. She went on to study art at Southwestern University in Kansas and achieved a double major in art and education.

Right out of college Juanita had an interview with Hallmark cards. She had intended to accept the position but she said, "I ended up getting married and pregnant so Hallmark fell by the wayside." For the next six or seven years Juanita started teaching on military bases. Then she opened her own studio. She did a lot of shows and received numerous awards. Her notoriety brought the attention of an art magazine called Popular Ceramics.   She wrote columns on art projects and how to projects for eleven years.   Juanita also worked for a magazine called Arts and Crafts. She was hired to go out on the road and teach classes for them.

In between traveling and teaching classes Juanita had a daughter, a son and adopted a son, giving her three beautiful children who have now gifted her with nine grandchildren and four great grandchildren. Juanita's children are proud of her accomplishments. Her son Todd said to her one day "if anyone has made their mark on the world you sure have!"

Juanita did a lot of trade shows and people would ask her to come and teach at their studios. One couple from South Africa sponsored her to teach in Johannesburg. She remembers her young grandson Adam saying, "Grandma I don't want you to go to South Africa, a lion will eat you!" While she was in Johannesburg Juanita taught seminars and showcased her art. She says one of the highlights of her trip was flying in a helicopter and seeing jungle cats in the wild.

Juanita had won first place in a national art competition. Her prize was two weeks in Bali. Always a people person, Juanita not only showcased her art in Indonesia but made many new friends including Elizabeth Gant. Elizabeth invited Juanita to visit England. Never missing an opportunity, Juanita decided to take Elizabeth up on her offer and on the way home from South Africa Juanita went to England. She remembers England as being beautiful and historic. She said that at the time she visited there was a moratorium that if you build anything new it has to look old so even the new buildings had a look of history to them. Juanita said, "the roundabouts drove me crazy. One time I almost hit a truck because I was in the wrong lane. But I'm versatile, and I just wing it! I learned from my art that you constantly learn and just go with the flow. That's what keeps me young."

Juanita's advice is you are never too young or too old to learn. "I would suggest study what is interesting to you, learn and explore. I got my first award at the age of seven for a giraffe I painted. Age doesn't matter. I still take classes. You can always learn. I'll be 79 this year and it doesn't seem possible. I look back on all the things I've done the books I've written, the people I've met, the columns, the classes and I think it's all around my art. You just have to do what you love and learn to adapt. Today arthritis is teaching me to adapt but I still do my art!"

THE HEART SCAN

Creating art is a means of watching yourself closely for self-defeating ways you respond to the world around you. Your artwork will speak to you louder than words. Pay attention to the colors you use, the shapes, and the symbols and you will find a brand new alphabet that brings clarity and understanding to your personal issues and growth.

Several years ago, while working in private practice as an art therapist, I created the HeART Scan. The HeART Scan is a voyage of discovery that allows your subconscious to speak volumes through the images you accidentally create. This exercise is a direct way to make contact with your inner self and find meanings unique to only you. Just let your hands draw without thought of outcome. Let the piece flow and create itself. The important thing is to free yourself from thoughts and just flow with the color.

- Avoid realism so you don't have to think about what you're drawing - just fill the paper with color and shapes.
- Choose your colors with your non-dominant hand and your eyes closed. This will allow you to choose colors without thinking. You can open your eyes and use your dominant hand to create your HeART Scan.
- Hang your finished picture in a place where you can look at it and study the different shapes and objects that you find. You will be surprised at what manifests.

CHAPTER 6
RENAISSANCE WOMAN
ARIANA NOLAN

"J'aime la vie. I feel to live is a wonderful thing."
Coco Chanel

When I was studying in Belize with a Mayan shaman my teacher told me, "Judith if you don't like your story, turn the page and write a new chapter." Ariana has done just that. She never settles. She knows what she wants and deserves. Ariana reminds us that when unexpected circumstances come our way they don't have to be viewed as problems or obstacles but rather a means for personal growth and expansion. It's our perception of things that change our reality. There is a yin and yang to everything and we have the power to choose either the negative or positive of any given situation. Whenever circumstances tried to bring Ariana down she moved forward with gusto. She is a testimony that life is what we choose it to be.

Thank you Ariana for reminding us we always have a choice. As for me, I choose to be happy.

"Don't think about the totality of the rest of your days. Just focus on now, allow yourself a little peace. You'll be surprised how easily "nows" can add up when you focus on them as they come." anonymous

ARIAN NOLAN

"A Renaissance woman is curious about the world and determined to keep learning throughout her lifetime. " (anonymous) Ariana Nolan is a true Renaissance woman. From the very beginning she has lived her life with honor and faith in her authenticity.

She was born and raised in the San Fernando Valley, until her parents moved to Rosamond in the Antelope Valley in 1954. Ariana said she hated Rosamond back then, so she went to live with her grandparents in Van Nuys, where she stayed until she got married right after high school. It wasn't a happy marriage. Her husband treated her like property with no respect for her individuality, and constantly reminded her that she was nothing without him. The free spirit in Ariana rose up and with her baby in tow, she left that marriage. This woman knew that she deserved to be respected and treated right. She set on a quest to be herself and restore her own authenticity.

While going through her divorce, Ariana secured a job at Capitol Records as a secretary. The Beatles were just getting popular and her department handled Beatles fan mail. Ariana's boss gave her tickets to a party for celebrities to bring their children to meet the Beatles. Here, Ariana had her picture taken with the 'fab four' and even received tickets to the Beatles' first Hollywood Bowl concert. Later, she met Bobby Darin and soon became his secretary.

"My ex husband always told me I could never get a job. I sure showed him!," she says, with a smile. "But remarkably, we stayed friends. That's just the way I am."

"Through it all, I have had many hats," Ariana recalls. "At one point I was in between jobs and didn't know how I would survive. I happened across The Power of Positive Thinking, and through reading that book, I learned to look for the good in everything. When I see a tree I look at the structure and harmony of the tree and see its beauty. That carries over into everything in my life. I only remember the good and always strive to keep a positive attitude. And Life always provided a new opportunity for me."

In 1968, Ariana moved to Palm Springs and soon got a job as a waitress. While waiting tables, she met a man who was in real estate. He told Ariana he would hire her if she got her real estate license. Ariana went back to school, became a realtor and went on to get her broker's license. She successfully sold real estate in the Palm Springs area for several years during the cooler seasons, and went to work as a waitress at the Sahara Tahoe during the summers.

In 1972, Ariana moved to Sacramento because she wanted to pursue a college education. Her son was in high school, and Ariana enrolled at American RIver Jr. College and then at Sacramento State University, where she studied art and photography. She continued working in Tahoe in the summers for the necessary money to put herself through school. After graduation, Ariana got a job managing an art gallery, and then began traveling, selling her own paintings at various art shows. She visited the Bay Area, Utah, Arizona, and Nevada, and did three or four shows a month.

"It was so much fun," said Ariana, "I started living the artistic life and freed myself to go in a new direction. It always provided enough to get by. I never did without."

Ariana lived the artistic dream until 1994. Her parents were getting elderly so she moved back to Rosamond where her son and his two children also lived. She started taking care of her parents and helped raise her grandchildren. Once again she was going in a new direction. In her free time, Ariana took art classes, dance classes, joined a book club, and took computer classes at Antelope Valley College. Photography was always a hobby and another outlet for her artistic eye, from her days in Palm Springs, when she would take pictures of real estate, and even photograph the occasional wedding, through to the present. And as busy as she was, Ariana also started raising dogs, developing her own breed which she called "Schmoodles". They were a cross between Shih Tzu, Maltese and Poodle.

"I really loved raising the animals, socializing them and loving them. I would hold the babies everyday, pet them and talk to them." Her puppies were always in demand and she had orders for them even before they were born.

Ariana's two grandkids and four great grandkids still live close to her in Rosamond. She enjoys doing things with them and sharing all of her adventures.

"My life has been in stages," she remembers, "Secretary, waitress, real estate agent, photographer, student, artist, dog-breeder, and caregiver. Every time I got good at something, a new idea or opportunity would appear on the horizon. Whatever I did, I gave it my all. When you're doing the best you possibly can, that's always good enough. I never ruthlessly tried to benefit from others. I always wanted everyone to win, and I contributed my full share for the good of the people I worked with. All through my life, I've held up my head and have done my best." She pauses to think. "And I've always been close to nature and to God. Growing up I had a deep relationship with Spirit. I enjoyed solitude, and just feeling God's presence. I knew that He always protected me. I never had a lot of money but I was always alright. Because of my relationship with God, I have never felt alone. I have been single for forty years but I am never alone."

And that, my friends, is a life well lived. Thank you, Ariana, for all you've done, for all you still do, and for all the many gifts you continue to share with our community.

CREATE A SAFE PLACE FOR YOUR EMOTIONS

1. Take some time to center yourself and think about things that make you happy.
2. Ask yourself what colors and shapes come to mind when you think about your happy feelings.
3. Decorate a box or container with your happy colors and shapes. You have artistic license to make the box your own.
4. Take some time to center yourself once again and think about personal emotions or feelings that may be holding you back.
5. Write one of these emotions on a piece of paper. Your choice of words are personal to your life experiences.
6. On the other side of this piece of paper, write a word that means the opposite of that emotion.
7. Repeat steps 5 and 6 as many times as you want.
8. Place the papers that list your emotions in your box to keep them safe.
9. Take a paper out of your box whenever you feel the need.

CHAPTER 7
TEACHER, COUNSELOR, GIFT FROM GOD
JANE ZEOK

"Wisdom is one of the few things in life that does not diminish with age."
Ram Dass

What is a wise woman? Proverbs 31 describes her worth as far above rubies and says a wise woman is worth her weight in jewels. According to yourdicftionary.com, she is "a woman who is venerated for experience, judgment, and wisdom." Jane Zeok is a wise woman. Her gifts are vast and she's not afraid to share them with others. Because Jane has an understanding of life that is way beyond most, it is healing and comfortable to be around her. She's a very busy lady but always remembers to take time out to feed her soul because that's what a wise woman does. One of my Mayan teachers taught me that unless you make deposits into your spiritual account when you go to make a withdrawal there will be nothing there. Thank you Jane for reminding me of this basic truth. Jane's life is a testimony to the importance of recognizing your talents, wisdom and truth and living them to the fullest.

JANE ZEOK

Some people just have a way of naturally empowering others. The beauty of this is that your own power is not diminished in the process. Jane Zeok is one of those people. A strong woman, Jane always brings out the best in everyone she meets, and still stands tall in her own authenticity.

She was born on a farm in Kansas. When Jane was 13, her father found an opportunity to embrace the yen he'd always had to "go north". He heard about an irrigation project in Washington state, that was recruiting farmers, and decided to move the family. Jane remembers her friends being shocked because people really never moved away from that little community. They'd be giving up the family farm that had belonged to her grandfather. But move they did. Jane finished high school and college in Washington.

She met her first husband, Ed, in high school but it wasn't love at first sight. "He was a jock and I just wasn't interested. There were these cool guys in the next town of Moses Lake and they were from Southern California. My friends and I would get our parents' cars on weekends and head over to hang with them. I knew right then that I was meant to be a California girl." After high school, she attended Eastern Washington University, changing her major from psychology to sociology, which led her to become interested in the more specific field of criminology. Her psych club adopted the criminally insane ward at a local mental hospital, and visited there often. "These were some of the most fascinating people I'd ever met," she remembers. "Most of them were absolutely brilliant, and very, very cagey. They had a way of figuring out exactly what story you'd be most likely to believe, and then could spin you some real tales!" When Ed transferred to EWU, she introduced him to her circle of artistic friends. "In those days, the 'Beat Generation' had come into fashion. We had our own coffee shop downtown, and I'd stop by there periodically, in my black tights, miniskirt and beret, to hear my friends read poetry while someone played the bongos. I felt quite urban and avant garde," she laughs. Because she and Ed were from the same small town, he asked if she'd like to ride home with him once or twice a month, and so they became good friends. Eventually, that proceeded to what seemed the next logical step--marriage. "Of course, our parents felt we'd never finish college then, but there was never any doubt in my mind. When our son was born on our first wedding anniversary, the mantle of motherhood fell across my shoulders, and made me realize that I really needed to get serious about my future. Having changed my major several times, I would need to take more classes in one specific field in order to move into a particular career path. Ed wanted to be a teacher, and I saw that although it would take me another year to finish up the elementary education classes, it made the best possible sense for a viable career path. And since I'd taken French every year, it was another easy step to simply declare that as my major. So I graduated with a B.A. in Education and a major in French." After graduation, they were recruited by the Palmdale School District in 1964 and moved to California. Ed taught 6th grade, then became a vice principal, a principal, and ended his career as assistant superintendent of schools for the Palmdale District. Jane taught third grade for 2 years, and then stayed home for ten years, during which time their daughter was born. "I felt strongly about devoting myself to my children during their formative years," she says. When her daughter was eight and her son thirteen, she made the choice to return to her teaching career. She loved new challenges, and after a year or two in one grade, liked moving on to another, where developing a whole new creative curriculum awaited her. She taught 3rd, 4th, 5th and 6th, and then settled into several years as a language arts teacher at the intermediate school level. Almost every year, she had the gifted student cluster in her classrooms, and for a year and a half, she had the bilingual student cluster in her classroom as well. As with all of her students, these two groups provided rich opportunities to stretch her abilities to bring out that special, unique blossoming in each student. Eventually, she went back to school, during the evenings and on weekends, and earned her M.A. in school counseling, ending her career with twelve years as a school counselor. "That was an especially fulfilling time for me," she recalls. "Seventh and eighth graders are in a particularly challenging time in their lives, and they need people around them to really love, understand, and guide them. And I enjoyed getting back to my first love, psychology. I've always been intrigued by what makes a person tick, what has made them who they are."

Ed and Jane's marriage ended after 22 years. "I often said that we should have just remained good friends," she says. "Marriage put a strain on who we were as individuals, and what we each thought was significant in life. But it gave me tremendous impetus to continue improving and growing, and always trying to be better as a person. And it gave us two beautiful children which alone was blessing enough.' Jane's son works at Edwards Air Force base and her daughter is a British history professor at Cal Poly Pomona. "Both my children have powered through all their most difficult challenges, have developed amazing skills and abilities, and continue to pursue their life purposes with such grace. I've been immeasurably privileged to be their mother."

Jane's philosophy has been that every day has a gift for each of us, and every one has something special within them to be nourished and brought to life. She said it was her job as a teacher to look for the potential in children and to nurture that. "We learn everything in life in our relationships with others," she says, "and I felt that one of the most important things about children's school experience was to teach them to get along cooperatively with each other and to respect individual differences." A woman of deep spirituality, Jane always felt like people needed the freedom to explore who they were inside in order to live their best lives. Says Jane, "Several of my students told me I helped them to see their own special, individual gifts. That was my goal. I wanted to empower them."

Always a free spirit, Jane loved to dance and one May night while out with friends she met a 'dark and mysterious stranger,' fell in love, and they were married later that year, on New Year's Eve. Shortly after their marriage, they moved from the Lancaster-Palmdale area to a house on five acres, west of Rosamond. "My husband was a city boy from Pittsburgh, and wasn't at all sure he could handle life in the 'desert wilds,' as he called it. For me, it was a return to my country roots, and after a long work day, how peaceful it was, driving along the freeway from Palmdale, letting the day's cares fly away with each mile, until I got to my place of refuge." They were together for 13 years when he died of cancer. After his death, Jane began to travel more. "It took me a while to realize I could do whatever I wanted." She was on a year-round work schedule at her school, which allowed her to have 3 weeks off here and there throughout the year. She traveled to England three times, went on a Mexican Riviera cruise, and gave more time to pursue her explorations into areas of interest. She attended lectures, plays and concerts. She took more art and dance classes, and went to Teotihuacan in Mexico to study with Don Miguel Ruiz. She took classes in remote viewing with a former Army Intelligence Remote Viewer, and another time, went to sit at Joshua Tree Park with Dr. Steven Greer to look for UFOs. Traveling across our country, to New York City, New England, Washington D.C., New Orleans, visiting historical landmarks, as well as relatives in the Midwest, also gave her much pleasure. She joined the Center for Spiritual Living and was on their board of directors for two separate three-year terms. After attending a Friendship Bridge fundraiser, she felt called to join that organization, which provided microcredit loans to the indigenous women of Guatemala. She visited Guatemala on an Insight Trip, to see for herself how the program worked.

"I still cry when I think of those little industrious women, working so hard to grow their cottage industries and care for their families. They can improve their lives so much with just a small loan, just a little hand up." She believes that we all have to find ways to give back, when our lives have been so abundantly blessed.

After retirement, it took awhile for Jane to learn to relax, unwind and slow her frenetic pace. Her spiritual practices, especially meditation and journaling, helped, as well as her T'ai Chi classes. She spent 10 days in Oaxaca, Mexico, with a friend who introduced her to artists, potters and weavers there, a very enriching experience. In 2014, she took another eye-opening tour, this time for 3 weeks in India. Later, she traveled to Ireland, Wales, England (again), and France. Jane's elder granddaughter, Nicci, lives in England, with her Air Force husband and their three children, and Jane is inordinately proud of her. Despite many moves and giving birth to her three lovely children, Nicci has managed to complete her college degree and get her M.A. in counseling. Jane's two younger grandchildren are equally accomplished.

They both went to French-American schools in their elementary years, so are bilingual. Presently, they attend Orange County School of the Arts, where Maia is in the acting conservatory and Cian the classical voice conservatory. They are socially aware and engaged, active in sports and school functions, and sing in the Royal School of Church Music choir at their Episcopal church. "My three grandchildren and my three great-grands are simply astounding. They are all so lively, full of personality and charm and brilliance. It's such fun to watch them grow and develop and shine. And of course, no other grandmother has ever said that about her own grands and great-grands," she adds with a wink.

Jane's advice to the younger generation is to just keep going. "I always did the next thing in front of me to do. It seems so incredible now, looking back, how I seemed to rather innocently take the next step. I think we're all inherently guided along the way. We all come to those places in life where we hit a wall. But then guidance arrives, a way opens up, we figure out how to surmount every seeming obstacle. And we learn with each step." She reminds us that we are all remarkable divine-humans and that it is important that whatever life brings, we pursue our dreams, never give up on ourselves, and never stop growing. Said Jane, "Life is an adventure, full of astounding opportunities. Even when I thought I'd never survive something, I was grateful later, for every moment, because every experience taught me something new. It's all just an amazing and wonderful journey. Live it fully!"

GO FOR THE GOLD - CREATE A MANDALA

If you seek a higher understanding of things you must first lay a solid foundation and establish a good balance in your life. The circle is balance, equality and unity. The mandala is the most commonly known form of sacred art. The mandala is often used as a tool for focusing the mind.

The word mandala is from Sanskrit and means mystic or sacred circle. Carl Jung taught that mandalas are an outer representation of our inner selves. Jung used mandalas to give creative form to his inner conflicts. He believed mandalas help us grasp the elusive understanding of our inner worlds.

To begin, find a quiet space and start at the center of your paper and move out from there. Use this exercise as a direct way to make contact with your inner self. Go inside and find meanings unique to only you. You will find that this exercise will lighten tension and bring insight to questions or issues.

"Each person's life is like a mandala - a vast, limitless circle. We stand in the center of our own circle, and everything we see, hear and think forms
the mandala of our life."
Pema Chodron

1. Close your eyes and take a deep breath to calm yourself and relax.
2. Make a list of all the things that you want to explore.

3. Pick three or four things from your list and think of a picture or symbol that represents each of them.
4. Use colored pencils or markers and draw a design in the center of a circle.
5. Add symbols or pictures from the list you created.
6. Try to repeat your pattern. If you place a symbol on one side draw the same symbol on the other side.

When you are done as you study your completed mandala answer the following questions in your journal:

Are there any repeated patterns?

Do I see any clues or messages that answer my initial question?

How did I feel while doing this exercise? What emotions arose?

CHAPTER 8
A WOMAN OF MANY HATS
ANDI HICKS

"The secret of genius is to carry the spirit of the child into old age, which means never losing your enthusiasm."
Aldous Huxley

The gifts that Andi Hicks brings to the table are enthusiasm and energy. She is contagious and wonderfully so. Andi just keeps going and going and going. She's always there to help others and always motivates them with her perseverance and tenacity. Andi gets things done but she doesn't do it for you she just highlights the fact that it's possible for you to do it yourself.

That's Andi, always giving, always caring and always there when you need her. Sometimes it seems Andi knows what you need before you do. Watching her life and example proves that there is no obstacle that can't be overcome.

"There is real magic in enthusiasm. It spells the difference between mediocrity and accomplishment."
Norman Vincent Peale

A woman wears many hats in one lifetime why shouldn't one of them be a crown?"
Annie Jones, Author

ANDI HICKS

Andi Hicks deserves a crown. The list of her hats is astonishing.

Executive Director at the Mary Pickford Institute for Film Education

Information Developer

Executive Secretary in Beverly Hills

Graphic Designer

Thoroughbred Breeder at Rancio della Gran Torre in Barbertown, New Jersey

Screenwriter

Editor of Expedition, The Magazine of the Americas

June Taylor Dancer

Broadway Stage (performed in seven Broadway Musicals)

Actor

Freelance writer

Mother, wife, honor student

And these are just the highlights!

Andi Hicks was born in New England. At the age of eighteen, after graduating high school with honors as the valedictorian of her class, she got on a bus to spend the summer in New York studying ballet. She wanted to stay forever but had earned a four-year scholarship to Boston State University to study nursing. Not long into her studies, Andi realized nursing wasn't her path and she switched her major to theater.

"The program was filled with these wonderful bohemian theater people," Andi remembers. "And I had realized that I wanted to be a New Yorker. I made the dean's list my first year of college, which gave me the incentive to apply to the American Academy of Dramatic Arts and move to New York."

During her second year at the academy, Andi went for an audition as a dancer. She got the job and gave up acting. She did several shows on Broadway and all over the East Coast, as well as making appearances in many commercials. On her 28th birthday, Andi felt she was "too old" to dance. Little did she know then that she would still be dancing well into her 70s. However, when Andi married, her life did change for a time, and she said good- by to Broadway.

Her new husband bought her a horse for her birthday. They moved to New Jersey and started a horse farm. That's where Andi learned to breed thoroughbreds. She also grew soy beans which wasn't popular because the rest of the farmers in the area grew corn. One of their farm workers, Carlos, was from El Salvador. Carlos suggested Andi and her husband vacation in his hometown of San Salvador This they did, but while they were gone tragedy struck. Their house burned and the crops failed. There was nothing left. But their El Salvador trip had provided rich ground in which new ideas could sprout.

Andi was never one to give up easily. With the help of her mom, she and her husband bought a travel trailer. They hit the road for Florida first. The plan was to go on an expedition - an American family engaging in trade and travel. Her husband was an excellent promoter and they received one hundred fifty thousand dollars in aid and products simply by writing a one page letter explaining their plan. In March 1977 they set off on an adventure they hoped would take them to Tierra del Fuego. While in Belize, they started a magazine. Andi learned hot press, lead printing, etching, and with her IBM typewriter, they published the journal, *Expedition, The Magazine of the Americas* to document their travels. When they got to Honduras they realized they had to settle for awhile due to the turmoil and strife in the region. Andi's husband got a job as principal of the American School. Unfortunately, he had faked his credentials, and when the government found out politely asked him to leave. Andi was left alone in Honduras with their four-year-old daughter. She couldn't leave Honduras until she settled their financial debts. Worried about her daughter's safety, Andi sent the child back to the States to live with her mother. Andi's husband learned that his daughter was in New England, kidnapped her, and moved to California.

It took Andi six months to get out of Honduras. She flew home, hired a private detective, found her daughter, kidnapped her back and negotiated for California joint custody. Because Andi was given joint custody, she had to stay in California. She got a job at IBM and was there for nine and a half years. During those years, Andi learned graphic design, computer graphics, and became an information developer. She married again but her new husband wouldn't let her do theater. He told her, however, that she could be a screenwriter. "I warned him that if I went back to writing he would lose me because writing is so all encompassing. Five years later I married my UCLA instructor Neill Hicks," said Andi. Screenwriting school was a productive period for Andi. She produced, directed and wrote several plays and documentaries.

Shortly thereafter, Andi became reacquainted with one of the dancers she had previously worked with on the East Coast. Her friend convinced her she could work again, and they started dancing in LA. Andi said it took her about five years because she was older, but now she's back in the theater, still answers casting calls, and recently landed a spot in another movie.

Neill and Andi moved to Tehachapi in 2002. Andi says while she misses a lot of the New York life, she likes the arts community in Tehachapi, having four seasons, and the interesting history. She says, "I think about all the things I'm doing now that I've not let myself do before, like teach and write and join theater groups, and most recently, the art of mixed media, and how it just...happens. That's been my life story. You just do it. It's beautiful. I just do it." Her advice to others is that, "Nothing is either good or bad. Thinking makes it so. Things don't happen for the best; you make the best of what happens." And she admonishes, "Communicate, because people don't know what you want, who you are and what you need unless you tell them."

Thank you Andi, for your story, your legacy, and the beauty and joy you bring to everyone you meet. You've allowed your life experience to evolve in many directions, and it is amazing how your strength and determination have always prevailed. That alone provides so much inspiration to many.

SELF-ESTEEM COLLAGE

Supplies:
- Card stock
- Magazines
- Glue
- Scissors

Directions:
1. Cover the card stock with a piece of colored background cut from a magazine.
2. Glue a circle in the middle of the page with the words "I AM".
3. Find positive words you believe about yourself or positive qualities you possess.
4. You can use words cut out from magazines or words you type on the computer.
5. Place your words around the "I AM" circle in the middle.

CHAPTER 9
A LIFE GUIDED BY
ROCK SOLID PRINCIPLES
SUSANNA MONETTE

"Do the right thing. It will gratify some
people and astonish the rest."
Mark Twain

One thing I've learned from Susanna is do it right the first time. Not one to shock people or attract attention, Susanna moves forward slow and steady. In addition to being a gifted artist, she is organized and competent and always gets the job done. It's inspiring to watch her because as an artist myself, organization is not one of my strong points. The other thing watching Susanna has taught me is not just to keep on keeping on but to be deliberate in my efforts. By moving in a meaningful direction things are bound to be successful. But most of all, the thing about Susanna is you can count on her. That's not a quality that is found in everyone.

Thank you Susanna. You truly remind us of what it means to be honorable.

SUSANNA MONETTE

Born in New York, New York, Susanna Monette grew up on the East Coast. She went to college in Wisconsin where she studied psychology. After graduation, Susanna moved to Chicago and landed a job with Neilson Ratings. She created graphs and presentations for the company's use in educating clients. Creating charts to provide the user with at-a-glance information wasn't easy in pre-computer days. Susanna's ability to impart critical information quickly and clearly is a testament to her attention to detail and her fine discernment, rapidly seeing how to assess the needs of others.

After the job at Neilson, Susanna worked for 17 years with Blue Cross of Illinois. During that time Susanna married and had a son, Randy. Susanna then got a job at Met-Life. It was the infancy of HMO marketing and she managed claims. When her husband died in 1989, Susanna moved to Las Vegas and worked for Sierra Healthcare Network. Eventually she took her skills as a claims adjuster to Arizona where she also opened a gift shop. She started playing around with polymer clay, took some sculpture classes, and learned loom beading and tie-dye. Susanna says she is largely self-taught. Whenever she wants to learn something she reads about it until she has a firm grasp of the technique. The gift shop was fun but grandkids are more fun, and Susanna moved to

Lancaster to be near her son Randy, who now has two children.

She met Cathy, her partner for the last ten years, at the Unitarian Church in Lancaster. They bought a home in California City and have been there ever since. Susanna became affiliated with Gallery and Gifts in Tehachapi, and in 2009 joined with Mel White at Crossroads. Together they started the Treasure Trove in 2012. The Treasure Trove has since become a community-gathering place. Susanna remembers the beginning when they were painting the walls. She said when they got to the back stairs she took some cans of paint and put rainbow footprints going up the steps to the attic. They are still on the steps today, a whimsical testimony to Susanna's artistic imagination. As part owner of the Treasure Trove in Tehachapi, Susanna's skills as a keen observer with concentrated awareness are essential and well appreciated. She's one of those people you can consistently depend on to get the job done.

Susanna's favorite thing about Tehachapi is the Loop. She loves trains. When she lived in Chicago she took the train everyday to work, and in the winter she always took the train home to the East Coast to visit family. One of her favorite places to visit is the train museum in San Diego, where they have an amazing diorama of the Loop. In addition to riding the rails, Susanna likes to read, and often attends Spirit Wind at the Community Church.

Her advice to others, especially young people, is to be active and stay healthy. Says Susanna, "It is very important to be active and do something besides TV and video games. Keep your body moving and your mind active. It makes a difference."

And Susanna Monette, you have made a difference in all the many lives you touch daily. Tehachapi thanks you.

Exercise in finding your authenticity:

Part I

1. For the next twenty minutes or so answer the question "When have I been the happiest and why?"
2. Do not think about what you want to say or how you want to say it. Just write.
3. Look at your list. What do the items have in common? What were you doing? Do you see any patterns?

Your list will answer the question "Who am I?" The person that you are becomes clear in your happy moments. When you're happy you are being yourself without worry. This is the real you. This is when you remember you are a conscious being.

Part II

1. Read through your list and answer the question: What is not present in my list? i.e. think about different people, your surroundings, the way you look.....
2. Look at your new list. What or who was not present at your happiest times?
3. It is important to recognize patterns in your answers.

Example: "I was rarely at work. or "Some form of art or music appears in most of my happiest moments."

The more time you are willing to spend analyzing your list, the more you will understand your hidden beliefs. Whatever you believe, not think, determines your reality. Your thoughts reflect your beliefs. Changing your thoughts alone will not improve the quality of your life unless you improve the beliefs behind your thoughts.

CHAPTER 10
TEHACHAPI'S BENEVOLENT ARTIST
MARILDA WHITE

"No one has ever become poor by giving."
Anne Frank

Mel White helps others see the world differently. Why? Because Mel is one of those people who is always reaching out to help others. She has consistently shared her art and expertise with the community not just in creating galleries and studios but establishing gathering places for fellowship and growth. It's a gift that keeps on giving. The cool thing is that Mel has taught me by giving to others you become a better version of yourself. For that I am grateful. Helping others without personal gain is a trait to be cherished.

MARILDA WHITE

"To do more for the world, more than the world does for you - that is success." Henry Ford

Marilda White, aka Mel, was born in Iowa in 1948. Her dad was in the Navy so she grew up all over the United States. She remembers going to six different grade schools. Mel says, "My parents had wheels for feet and we were constantly moving". You'd think constantly changing schools and homes would have made Mel introverted, but on the contrary, she became outgoing and resilient. In high school she received an award as the most valuable senior, in GRA, vocal, band and theater. Her loving and open personality continues to draw others to her to this day.

Mel earned a Bachelor of Science in recreational education and used her degree to follow many paths. She administered a home ownership program for low-income people in Colorado, worked with the big sister program in Marin County, and always gravitated to social service organizations and work that helped other people. Later, she went into journalism, writing for newspapers and periodicals. She has had a couple of books published, and her short stories have appeared in numerous magazines, including Sunset Magazine. Mel says one of her favorite jobs was working for newspapers covering sports events. Her father was an amateur photographer and shared his love for photography with Mel. She loved to take pictures, and she combined her talent with the camera and journalism as she conquered the field. Currently, she has a regular column in Tehachapi's Loop.

In 1986, her parents moved to Tehachapi. Mel was living in Denver then and visited irregularly.   Her dad became ill in 2000, and Mel came to the valley to help her family. She always thought she would settle up north, but a week after her dad died, Mel's mom was diagnosed with cancer. Mel stayed in Tehachapi and has been here ever since. She says she loves the scenery, the small town feeling, the wildflowers, and the four seasons. And most of all, Mel says, "The people here are some of the best people I've ever met. Even though I planned to just come and help my family, I'm glad I stayed. My mom and I were very close and shared so many memories. Tehachapi became more than home for me." After the death of her mom in 2003 and her sister Sandra in 2004, Mel had to decide what to do. She had established herself with Gallery and Gifts, and now was deciding whether to travel or to continue in Tehachapi, pursuing the arts. Mel had always been adventurous. She had previously done many cross-country trips, has always loved to drive, and once, she even rode her motorcycle through eight states on the way to Iowa.

"I love the idea of driving and going somewhere. I especially love weekend trips and day trips," said Mel. Fortunately for the residents of Tehachapi, Mel put travel aside for a season and chose the arts.

She hooked up with fellow artist Pat James. Together they envisioned a privately owned cooperative, which showcased local artists and held classes. In 2004, Mel rented a place with a yard and held lots of outdoor activities. It soon became a local hotspot known as The Tehachapi Art Center. One of the artists at the art center wanted a "real gallery". She talked Mel into opening Crossroads in 2005, which was a dedicated fine art gallery. After the opening, they started First Friday in conjunction with the Tehachapi Art Center. Mel says she hasn't missed a First Friday since they began in 2006. She even scheduled her recent knee surgery around the First Friday date to make sure she could attend.

Then in 2012, along with three of the artists from Crossroads, Mel established another gift to the community. They closed Tehachapi Art Center and Crossroads, and combined them to open the Tehachapi Treasure Trove.

"It is more than just an art center; it's full of treasures!" said Mel. "I get so excited when someone paints their first picture, sells a painting or learns a new skill. It's all about people supporting people. I like it when people are encouraged to try things and do things. The bottom line and what's really important is that people can feel safe. The Treasure Trove has become like a family. This is where I meet the most important people in my life."

Mel's advice to others is, "If there is something you want to do just do it! Even if people tell you it won't make you money. Time is precious and everything can turn on a dime. You just have to go for it. Just do it!"

And that's exactly what Mel White has done. Her vision has become a composite reality of all her travels, journeys and interests. And that vision has become a true gift to all of us.

Exercise: Find the Stillness

Find the stillness - ask yourself the following three questions
and journal the answers:

- What makes it difficult for you to take time to get
  emotional support for yourself?
- How was emotional release treated when you were
  young?
- How did adults treat you when you expressed your
  feelings?

1. Play some music and begin to draw whatever comes to
   your mind after answering the above questions. Let
   your hands do the work. Pick colors at random. Flow
   with the music and the supplies.
2. When you are done place the picture where you can
   view it and meditate on your images.
3. Use your intuition to guide you. What difference do you
   think it would make in your life if you regularly took time
   to release emotions?

CHAPTER 11
LOVING, COMPASSIONATE, INSPIRING
PATRICIA BUTLER

"A happy family is but an earlier heaven."
—George Bernard Shaw

Meeting Patricia Butler was a reminder of the importance of family. Mother Theresa said, "If you want to bring happiness to the whole world, go home and love your family." Patricia does just that and her joy is contagious. I only met her once but I was so impressed with the contentment and peaceful aura she presented. As we talked during the interview the importance of her family was apparent. She is a practical woman who cares for herself and those around her.

"Family isn't always blood. It's the people in your life who want you in theirs; the ones who accept you for who you are. The ones who would do anything to see you smile and who love you no matter what."
Anonymous

PATRICIA BUTLER

"To us, family means putting your arms around each other and being there."
Barbara Bush

"In family life, love is the oil that eases friction, the cement that binds closer together, and the music that brings harmony."
Friedrich Nietzsche

Patricia Butler moved to Bear Valley when her husband retired five years ago. Patricia was only seventeen when she married her husband.

"He fell in love instantly and finally won me," she laughs. At first, I wanted nothing to do with him. I had to decide between him and another guy. After a Thanksgiving open house with our family, he did the dishes. That impressed me so much I picked him, and I've never been sorry. We've been together 56 years!" Together they have five children (four still living), fourteen grandchildren, and seventeen great grandchildren. To Patricia, family is important. As modern life becomes more and more hectic and demanding, the benefits of living in a family are more important than ever.

"I don't know what I would do without my family," she says. "To me, family is everything. And in Tehachapi the whole community raises the kids. Everybody helps. You can actually drive down the street and people will wave."

A California girl, Patricia was born in LA and raised in Manhattan Beach. She grew up with a love for the ocean, and was a surfer girl in her youth. She remembers the day that she was riding the waves and someone hollered, Feet up!" She saw a big thing swimming underneath her, and said that was her last day of surfing.

Patricia also loves the mountains and all of nature. "Trees are God's greatest creations," says Patricia. "I also like growing things. One day a neighbor gave me some acorns. I planted them and grew about forty oak trees. I gave them to a gardener. He said he had never seen anyone grow trees like I did. When we lived in Rancho Margarita in Orange County, I had a ficus tree on the front porch. Twin hummingbirds visited for two years in a row and even built their nest in that tree."

Gardening isn't all that has kept Patricia busy. She said her mother crocheted all the time, and her brother and sister were "very artsy". She did ballet and tap for eight and a half years. She says she could never keep still.

"It started with my feet and to this day, I always keep my hands busy." One year, Patricia won second place in the State Fair with some of her crocheted pieces, and has well over 100 ribbons and awards from LA County and Orange County fairs. She loves to use recycled and repurposed items, making all sorts of crafts that she shares with others.

"Did you know that if you put pine cones in a glass jar with bleach for a couple of days, they will turn white?" Patricia asked. She uses those pinecones around the holidays to adorn gifts and create festive decor.

Holidays are magical at the Butler's house. "My husband says at Christmastime, I melt his credit cards. But it's worth it. We have a great family Christmas. And Thanksgiving is fun too. I usually cook for thirty some odd people and they are all family. My daughter's first husband and his wife even come. We all love each other and we are still one family."

Patricia's advice about life is to not always follow your heart because it can confuse you.

"Make sure you think about it," she advises. You can't lead with either the brain or the heart; you have to use both. Mind and heart go hand in hand. It gives you a deeper sense of meaning and connection to everything you do. They really should teach logic in school."

CREATE A JOY MAGNET

Supplies:

- heavy paper or cardboard
- colored markers
- craft magnets
- glue

Directions:

1. Think of two words
2. Create a new word out of the two words you chose

   Examples: abundant/peaceful = fullbunda

   healthy/energetic = energeal

   lack/prosperity = prosperack

   work/play = orkpla

3. You will know you landed on something when your word makes you smile.

4. Cut your heavy paper or cardboard into a fun shape.

5. Write your new word in the center of your shape.

6. Decorate your shape with colored markers.

7. Add a magnet to the back of your shape and place on the refrigerator.

ENJOY YOUR NEW WORD!

CHAPTER 12
A CONSTANT IN THIS CHAOTIC WORLD
NANCY WALDRON

"Patience and perseverance have a magical effect before which difficulties disappear and obstacles vanish."
John Quincy Adams

In psychology patience is used to refer to the character trait of being steadfast. Whatever situation she encounters, Nancy Waldron exhibits strength and stability. No matter the task, in her own quiet way she gets the job done in a seemingly effortless manner. Thank you Nancy for reminding us that the ability to follow life's natural rhythm and let things flow is a trait worth seeking.

"He that can have patience can have what he will."
Benjamin Franklin

NANCY WALDRON

"I long to accomplish a great and noble task, but it is my chief duty to accomplish small tasks as if they were great and noble." Helen Keller

Nancy Waldron has lived in Tehachapi since 1998, when her job in Northern California transferred her to Bakersfield. Nancy said she has always lived near mountains so she chose Tehachapi as her base. She has never regretted her decision. She loves the four seasons, the small town feel, the friendly people, and most of all, the art community.

Nancy's mother was a girl scout leader and she instilled in Nancy a love for crafts. In the 80s, Nancy learned tole painting and, along with her mother, took oil painting classes. Nancy soon found she liked acrylics better and painted on everything she could find, even saws. Her work was popular and she sold at shows and art fairs. After moving to Tehachapi, she studied with David Rheinhart and watercolor became her favorite medium.

Says Nancy, "Watercolor is a passion for me. It teaches patience. The layers have to dry in-between just like in life. When I paint in my studio by myself I'm in my own little meditative world."

Her words are a valuable reminder, in our often fast-paced world, to stay grounded in our own stillness, trusting the process to move us to a perfectly crafted outcome. Patience is a virtue.

Nancy grew up in San Jose, California. She met her husband on a 4th of July weekend. He came with friends but he and she were the only singles at the party. They started dating and got married in 1990. After their marriage, they moved to Morgan Hill. She worked for an insurance company until she retired. Her company often transferred her throughout her tenure. Nancy's husband was in construction and so was able to travel with her. The consistency of her career is most impressive. So many people want a big breakthrough or instant success. They may change jobs several times over the course of their working life. Nancy found it validating to stay with her chosen profession. In the process, she was rewarded with authenticity and the ability to continually break through to new areas of fulfillment. Her innate ability to follow life's natural rhythm and flow with the tide has enabled her to create a life where she is free to be herself in safety and joy. And now she is a loving and contributing member of our community. She has been with the Treasure Trove since they opened in 2012, and works there every Wednesday. She not only markets her art but often offers classes and workshops.

When she's not at home, she loves to travel. Nancy likes to go on vacations, which include art experiences. She has taken workshops around the US and Europe. Her favorite one was held in Italy and France. She brings home what she learns when she teaches new workshops and classes. Nancy loves to be around other artists and to expand her circle of friends. She says art is the highlight of her life and has always been a thread in everything she has done.

"I feel it is a healthy thing to do. It gives you confidence and empowers your self worth. I like to try new things. It keeps me learning and active."

Nancy's advice to others is to remain open to your ever-unfolding potential. She says even if you think you know it all and how things should be, you have to leave your horizons open and continue to try new things.

"If you don't limit yourself you will leave your mind open to unlimited potential. Be patient. The good things are worth waiting for."

CREATE A SYMBOL OF YOUR DESIRES AND BELIEFS

Supplies:
- Journal
- pen
- paper
- colored pens

Ask and answer the following questions several times each for your positive and negative thought patterns:

Negative thought patterns:

Write ten or more negative motivations that describe why you resist doing well in your life. Example - "What I really want is …..to hide away from the world for fear of criticism."

Positive thought patterns:

Write ten or more positive motivations that you can think of that describe why you authentically want to do well in your life. Example - "What I really want is ….to do well financially so that I can buy a house."

RELEASING LIMITING BELIEFS

1. Identify a limiting belief that you would like to clear. Close your eyes and imagine a picture or symbol for your limited belief. Draw your image in your journal.
2. Breathe deeply and find where your body contract and what emotions you feel when you repeat your negative belief.
3. Breathe into each contracted area of your body. One at a time, talk to each contracted area and tell it that your limited belief is not true.

4. Tell your body to relax and let go of the contraction.
5. When your body begins to relax imagine your limited belief and symbol again and stamp it with "Canceled". Write "Canceled" over the top of your negative belief symbol in your journal.
6. Sit back, contemplate your image and imagine what your life would be like without your limited belief.
7. Draw a new symbol that represents a healthy belief.

CHAPTER 13
CALM AND PEACEFUL PRESENCE
CAROL CASEY-NEWELL

In today's fast paced society it's hard to just sit still and rest the mind. Carol Casey-Newell brings stillness into her everyday. She has learned the best gift of all - to surrender and listen. She worked for several years as a therapist for adolescents, a caregiver for eight years with her first husband and now a caretaker of rescue animals. Life hasn't always been an easy road yet through it all this dynamic woman retains a calm and peaceful demeanor. Carol reminds us it's okay to just be.

"Many spiritual cultures agree inner stillness creates an energetic environment for supporting our advancing consciousness that can unleash the transformational power of our love." www.heartmath.com Whenever I'm around Carol-Casey Newell, I feel that love. I feel heard, I feel honored and I feel peaceful. Thank you Carol.

"Be still. Stillness reveals the secrets of eternity."
Lao Tzu

"So the darkness shall be the light, and the stillness the dancing."
T. S. Eliot

CAROL CASEY-NEWELL

Carol Casey-Newell always loved school. She attended Hayward State College, where her favorite courses were in art, especially drawing. She gave both structure and a solid foundation to her love of art by becoming an art therapist at Napa State Hospital. She worked mostly with adolescents and helped them discover the healing power of art.

After marrying a college professor, they made their home in Idaho. When he retired, he wanted to relocate, so they explored options. Carol's sister lived in Bakersfield and her son was in Temecula, so they came to California to check out the area. It seemed good to be closer to family, so in 2002 they decided to settle in Bear Valley. Carol said she likes being around nature. She loves the natural beauty and the open space of the community.

A year after the move, Carol's sister died. Then Carol's husband was diagnosed with dementia. Carol joined a caregivers resource group to help support her through this difficult time. When her husband passed away in 2008, she joined a grief counseling group at the Valley Resource Center. It was there she met her current husband, Hal. They were married in 2010.

Art is still a big part of Carol's life and she loves working in her home studio. Her appreciation of nature and open spaces moves Carol effortlessly to a deep love of horses, dogs and other animals. This has led her to foster rescue pets. She says that all of her dogs over the years have been rescue animals. She also enjoys volunteering at the California

Living Museum as a docent in their rehabilitation facility. The facility is an educational zoo but the primary focus is saving native species.

Her ability to work with animals isn't surprising because Carol is a dynamic woman with a calm and composed presence. She meditates often and says meditation helps her pause, reflect and stay in the moment. Carol shared an experience she had at the Vipasana Center in North Fork where she attended a ten day silence and reflection workshop. She said it was a wonderful time of silence and quieting the mind down. "It changed my life and taught me the importance of going within. That week brought me the greatest joy."

When asked if she had any advice for the younger generation, Carol replied, "Live in the moment. Appreciate the moment because it's not going to come around again." And she emphasized that meditation, that time of quieting the mind, stopping to be with the stillness, is key to being fully present in each moment.

"There's a point when your tape of life runs off the reel and there's this stillness of your own - I got to know myself."
-Melissa Etheridge

Inner Stillness Heart Meditation

(from www.heartmath.com)

Find a place to breathe quietly for a few minutes. (You can always find a place – close the door to your office or room, or the bathroom, or outside in a quiet area.)

Focus your attention in the area of the heart and pretend your breath is flowing in and out of the heart or chest area. With each breath imagine your mind, emotions and body getting still inside.

From that place of stillness, feel a caring connection with someone or a pet you are close to, or just focus on peace. Don't look for experience just be – without exploring your mind's inserts. This creates inner-coherence and a deeper connection with your heart's suggestions.

Gently excuse any thoughts that come up, positive or negative know that you can entertain them at another time. As thoughts come up, don't push against them; just casually focus on breathing love and peace into the stillness for a few minutes to anchor the feeling into your cellular memory.

Practicing inner stillness will help you recall the feeling more quickly when discerning important matters and directions.

CHAPTER 14
HER GIFT KEEPS ON GIVING
SUZI MC REYNOLDS

"Let the beauty of what you love be what you do."
Rumi

The thing about doing what you love is that you can share what you do with the world. That's exactly what Suzi Mc Reynolds has done her whole life. Sometimes we're not aware of how much we touch others just by living the life we love. The Dalai Lama says, "*I believe the very purpose of life is to be happy.*" He says that because happiness is contagious. If you're happy everyone around you is too!

And that's what Suzi McReynolds brings to the table. She has brought her creativity and love of art to all aspects of her life, through sewing and tailoring, real estate, gardening. She lives what she loves and that's the beauty and secret of her calm composure and spirit. I am a firm believer that art in any form helps heal the psyche and feed the soul. Suzi is a perfect example of the healing power of art. She has given us all a gift just by the life she lives.

"The meaning of life is to find your gift. The purpose of life is to give it away."
Pablo Picasso

SUZI Mc REYNOLDS

A California girl, Suzi McReynolds was born in San Bernardino. During her early childhood, she lived on a ranch in Lucerne Valley outside of Victorville, spent a few years in Long Beach and then the San Fernando Valley. When she was ten years old her family moved to Chino Valley in Arizona just outside of Prescott.

Her first job was making hamburgers but art was always her passion. However, her parents told her that art was too frivolous to be a career, so she went to nurses aide school. Suzi was a nurse's aide for three years and then worked as a physical therapist before joining a firm of land developers. The job eventually led her to Tehachapi in the early 70's on an airplane that landed in the Cummings Valley. The company was selling parcels in the area, and as a contract-writer, she came for a first hand look. It was love at first sight. She settled in Caliente, and then, in 1975, she moved to Tehachapi, which she says reminded her of Arizona.

Suzi was in her 20's when she moved to Tehachapi, with two young children, a girl and a boy. Unfortunately her early marriage hadn't lasted and she was now a single mom. Suzi's daughter is autstic, so in 1976 she moved her little family to Santa Barbara where there was a specialized program for autistic children at UCSB. Suzi was determined to give her daughter the best care possible. Life wasn't always easy but her strength saw her through the difficult times.

In Santa Barbara Suzi made her living as a seamstress. She was self taught and has been sewing since she was six years old. She remembers putting on fashion shows as a young girl. Suzi says she would make elaborate stages out of curtains where she would showcase her creations, made from the patterns she had drawn and sewed. She always wanted to do art and remembers looking at watercolors with a sense of yearning. "They spoke to my soul," Suzi recalls. "I just knew if I could have paints, I could do it." But life became so difficult, and she was too busy raising two children on her own to pursue her artistic talents. It wasn't until she was in her 50's that she started painting.

In 1982, Suzi felt the yearning to come back to Tehachapi. She said the lifestyle and the people in Santa Barbara were very transient, always coming and going, without that settled feeling of 'home'. Says Suzi, "I love Tehachapi. I love the oak trees, the rolling hills, the boulders, the deer and the wild life. The foxes are my favorite. They come up to me and sit with me. I love the outdoors. I walk between four and eight miles a day. I love gardening and being outside. Tehachapi is home."

Suzi lost her son when he was in his 30's. She said being in touch with nature was the thing that held her together during that difficult time. Suzi's daughter now lives in a special care home in Riverside. Her son had two boys and they live with their mom in Seattle.

After returning to Tehachapi Suzi worked in real estate. She helped the community for thirty-one years. Suzi recently said, "I used to think I wasn't doing what I wanted because I really loved art. But one day I figured out I was doing art by helping people. I helped people design their homes, stage their homes for selling and I helped young people get their first home." In the community everyone called her Suzi Mac. To this day she is still well loved and remembered for all the gifts she shared over the years. She made a difference in the lives of a lot of people. We salute you Suzi Mac!

And Suzi is still doing art. She finally mastered watercolors and sells her paintings at the Treasure Trove. Some of her favorite things to paint are the signs she sees all over town. She captures them first in photographs and then paints them in wonderful watercolors. Her beautiful greeting cards are also available, and she loves to create hand-painted postcards to send to her two grandchildren.

Suzi's advice to others is "Do what you love!" To young people, especially, she says, "Go to school. Even if you don't like it, get a good education so you can do whatever you want."

HANDMADE BOOK OF ME

Complete each phrase to help in your journey of self-discovery.

I am (first name, last name)

I wonder

I hear

I see

I want

I am

I pretend

I feel

I touch

I worry

I cry

I am

I understand

I say

I dream

I try

I hope

I am (first name, last name)

CHAPTER 15
AN OLD SOUL
JANICE PADGETT

Your visions will become clear only when you can look into your own heart. Who looks outside, dreams; who looks inside, awakes. Carl Jung

Janice's story comes from a long journey. She is an old soul. You don't have to explain it, it can't be put into words she just is - a loving beautiful, nonjudgmental gift to this world. She taught children, both her own and in the Greenfield School District, worked in the mental health field for many years, tended to her husband and her family, overcame dependencies and stands strong to this day as a testimony to love, peace and connection with the universe and an understanding of universal truth. She reminds us that what appears to be loss may in fact be transformation.

By touching the past with the present, she has risen with strength and fortitude. Janice reminds us that by liberating from our old roles we are gifted with a chance to seize an authentic way of being. I for one am glad that Janice Padgett has made her wisdom felt in this world. We are all blessed by her testimony.

When we do the best we can, we never know what miracle is wrought in our life, or in the life of another."

– Helen Keller

–

–

JANICE PADGETT

It wasn't until she went through the process of deep self-discovery and finding herself and that she was able to share all of her gifts with others. Janice Padgett has the spirituality of the universe and sees the connections between souls, people, and events that happen. She understands that we are all on individual journeys and each road is different. Some don't even know they are on a journey, or what their goal is. Janice seems to be blessed with the ability to go right to the source, recognize where she is, and thus help others find their way. When you ask her a question, she digs out information from her own personal and spiritual experience, and she is able to answer in a way that the questioner can easily grasp.   She has the gift of touching the greater scope of our existence. It's a wonderment to her as well as to the people who listen. She is truly a wise woman and an old soul, but didn't know that for the majority of her life.

A native California girl, Janice was born in Bakersfield. She says her early life was idyllic. The youngest of two children she grew up in Oildale during the time that it was a Standard Oil Company town. Janice remembers having the opportunity to experience an exceptional education there, with music, extracurricular activities, and privilege.   In high school, her boy friend was the student body president. They got married in 1964 and moved to San Jose where their first child was born. Janice and her husband both attended San Jose State. She wanted to pursue a degree in psychology It was the beginning of the flower child movement and the Vietnam War era. She was active in Another Mother for Peace, and lived a simple life with a loving heart and a kind soul.

Financial reasons caused the couple to move back to Bakersfield. They were able to purchase a home that needed to be restored. Janice remembers living in their first old house. "We were both highly creative, and worked our tails off with that first restoration," she said. "Then we moved to another old house, and continued fixing up and flipping houses."

After her second child was born, she didn't want to work full time, but did begin to volunteer at a mental health facility. Eventually they hired her, and she worked with occupational therapy in the activities department. Janice loved her job but both she and her husband missed the Bay area. They were able to sell their house and move back to the ocean.

"My oldest son was in the second grade and my youngest was two when things began to go sour. We had married young and my husband was trying to recapture the youth he hadn't fully experienced. He made wrong choices, started using drugs, and then sleeping around. I didn't react very well," Janice recalled. "I hadn't come from divorce. My parents were happy, and I had been raised with the security of knowing I was loved," remembered Janice. She really didn't expect a divorce. Janice wanted counseling, and thought they would get through it. Her husband didn't concur. When she visited with a therapist, she was told, "You won't like going through a marital break-up but you're going to be okay."

Janice took the boys and drove back to Bakersfield. She said, "When I let myself slow down and experience it, it was like waves of labor contractions, almost like giving birth to a new life. As long as I could hold on and ride it out, it would get better almost like giving birth to a new life. I moved in with a friend for a while, and then I got a little house. My dad helped me fix it up. We settled into a new life. I was just living life looking out for my kids."

Janice had several good friends who wanted to fix her up with someone. She really didn't want to meet him but her friends insisted. They told her "Hey, you wear Birkenstocks and he wears Birkenstocks, he got married young and his wife left him. You both have had the same issues." Armed with the assurance that there was no obligation, Janice met him on a blind date at a friend's house. They connected and were married a year later. They've been together now for 44 years.

Together with her husband and their children, they built a home in Bear Valley. Janice said, "Bear Valley had all these activities for kids so we acted as our own contractor and built our house there." Her husband worked in the high school district, and Janice completed her education with a BA in psychology. She had always wanted to be a therapist, so began working towards her Masters. At this time, she had been working at a mental health center with developmentally disabled adults, but she applied for a job in Tehachapi with a company that had a contract with the department of corrections. She worked as a counselor to keep family connections intact. Janice said, "Everyone was great to me. I never had an issue there, but I decided not to finish my masters. All I saw was heartache and sadness. It was like looking at the other side of the rock, when you pick it up and see all that life crawling around."

At the same time there were problems at home. She said there were good things about her marriage, but also things that would never be resolved. She used alcohol to numb herself. Says Janice, "I didn't want to leave another marriage. I had survived putting and keeping things together by drinking a lot. I would drink to gain energy. I was just tired of being sick and tired. All marriages are a mixed bag. There are fantastic things and there are some things that are not so great."

Janice didn't get a divorce. She chose instead to change her life. She got help with her personal problems, went back to school, earned her teaching credential, and quit her job at the prison. Janice taught elementary school for twenty years in a School District in Bakersfield. Says Janet, "I wasn't real thrilled at home, but I could go to school where there were enough different little people and always someone worse off than me. My life began to be centered around the kiddies first. I loved to nurture them, teach them, and in turn, nurture myself."

Janice's advice to others is, "You have to have within yourself a certain amount of willingness to be honest, to drop the crap, and face yourself, whatever it is. No matter how bleak it looks, you still have to take that step, whether it's changing careers or staying sober or getting out of or into a relationship. It begins when you look at yourself."

I learned this exercise is from Dr. Jennifer Freed.

www.jenniferfreed.com

Dr. Freed is an author, speaker and consultant. She teaches learning strategies to bring more magic to your daily life.

DETECTIVE FOR A DAY

1. Pay attention and make a list of things you have not seen or noticed before in your familiar surroundings.
2. See others you know and discover something about them you have missed in small or big ways.
3. Look at yourself in the mirror and choose to see something in your face or character you have been overlooking.
4. Throughout the day, ask yourself *"What can I see in a new way right now?*
5. At the end of the day, lists the insights you have noticed and explore them in your journal.
6. Before you go to bed look in the mirror, wink and say to yourself *"I AM HOT!"*

Oh the places you'll go." Dr. Seuss

CHAPTER 16
SHERRIE ANN BEATEY HARRIS
SHE TRAVELED THE WORLD

When I first met Sherrie, I was so impressed with her vibrant personality. The joy in her spirit was contagious, and I wanted to be around her. At first notice, she seems so quiet and reserved, but once she starts talking it's like observing a beautiful flower opening up. She doesn't need to be in the limelight because she lives her light. And it's truly luminous.

Sherrie may be reserved and self-contained but that doesn't mean she is shy. Maybe it's her years of experience as an airline hostess or maybe it's her natural personality. Regardless of the reason, she exudes a quiet, thoughtful way of interacting with others. Her very essence has a calming, meditative effect that reflects inner peace and contentment.

"The more I see the less I know for sure." John Lennon

"Life is either a daring adventure or nothing at all"
Helen Keller

SHERRIE ANN BEATY HARRIS

Sherrie Ann Beaty Harris was born in Woodville, Texas. She was always a loner. She loved to read, she loved to discover new things, she loved art.

Her family lived on the outskirts of town and Sherrie entertained herself a lot. She knew how to make herself happy. Even though she grew up spending a lot of time on her own, Sherrie also knew how to hold a crowd and work the room. Her outgoing personality became an asset in later life.

Sherrie started her adult life as a bookkeeper for the gas company. In her early twenties, life changed when she was hired by American Airlines. She worked as an airline hostess for forty-five years. During layovers, she explored the towns she landed in. Sherrie said, "I had a ball being a tourist." When the airlines started doing military airlifts, Sherry began flying to Cambodia, with stopovers in Honolulu and Okinawa. She remembers the soldiers being amazing. "One young man was sleeping and when I touched him on the shoulder to let him know we were landing, he opened his eyes and said, 'Round eyes, I haven't seen round eyes in so long.' Sherrie said you had to be careful not to startle the soldiers because so many of the men were used to being in battle and if you woke them suddenly they might lunge at you.

After doing airlift command for eight years, American went international. Sherrie was delighted. She started flying to Australia and New Zealand and got to see a lot of the world. She loved to travel and was no stranger to adventure. In her early fifties she was still traveling, but finally decided she would like to have someone to share life with. Sherrie remembers thinking, "I wish I had a man in my life. It doesn't matter what he looks like, or what kind of work he does, just so he is kind." Shortly thereafter, a co-worker asked Sherrie if she would go out with her father-in-law, who she described as the kindest man on the planet. Sherrie thought to herself, "Where did I hear these words before!" and immediately agreed to meet him. It was love at first sight. He was a retired nuclear submarine commander. They were together for three years and then married. Eight months after the marriage, he died of complications from diabetes. A friend later asked Sherrie, when she was grieving, if she wished she hadn't met him because of the pain of losing him. "If I had never met him," Sherrie replied,"I would have never known how deeply I could fall in love nor how kind a human could be. Meeting him was the nicest part of my life."

Sherrie never married again. She thought the possibility of finding someone as special as her husband was highly unlikely. After retiring from the airlines, she settled in Hawaii for a season. Then, ten years ago, she started a whole new life, and moved to Tehachapi to live with her sister, Betty. Sherrie says that after seeing the world she loves it here--the people, the small town feeling, and the fact that when you come to town you always see someone you know. She also loves the quiet of the canyon, the wild creatures, and especially the ravens and coyotes. She spends time reading, creating, and revisiting her love for art. She enjoys painting and exploring different art mediums, and shares her work with others at the Treasure Trove.

Says Sherrie, "If you have any regrets when you're an old lady, make them regrets for what you didn't do, not what you did. Always explore, always look around. Find something new and don't be afraid to go with it."

RANDOM RELATIONS

This is a fun way to play with synchronicity. Look around the room and pick three objects. Think about how those three items might inform you about your current thoughts and feelings. What are the messages hidden within these random items?

Here are some other examples of ways to do this exercise:
1. Open a book to any page and pick a random word or sentence
2. Create a quick collage by gluing radom images or words onto a page
3. Turn on the TV or radio and listen to the first words spoken

*"Then you will know which way to go, **since you have never been this way before**…and the Lord will do amazing things among you" (Joshua 3:4-5).*

CHAPTER 17
BETTY FLORES
A WOMAN OF STRENGTH

Surefooted, stedfast, strong, tenacious, that's Betty Flores. She's a pioneer woman but she's also big hearted, loving, creative and full of love. It takes courage to let go and hold fast. It takes courage to trust in a higher power no matter what comes your way in life. Betty has weathered many storms and always comes out on both feet. She continues on course in spite of difficulties and as such is a testimony to a life well lived.

Betty is not afraid to be herself. She lives with the land, the wildlife and nature. She works with her hands, tending to her animals, creating art and sharing with others. You can find Betty's heartfelt art at the Treasure Trove in Tehachapi. Come to a class where she is a participant and you might go home with farm fresh eggs. Betty Flores lives her life in authenticity. You can rest assured that what you see is what you get. This beautiful woman remains true within and without.

"When you dance your own rhythm, life taps its toes to your beat."
Terri Guillemets

BETTY FLORES

Betty Flores was born in Orange, Texas. At the early age of five her parents moved to South Carolina and that's where she grew up. They lived on a farm away from the city. Betty had horses, animals, open spaces in which to roam, and solitude. She loved nature, and knew as soon as she could pick up a stick and draw in the dirt that art was her passion.

After high school, Betty followed her older sister to California. She settled in West Hollywood but had to leave her horses behind in North Carolina. She soon tired of traveling back and forth to care for her animals and finally with the help of her then husband, bought a ranch in the San Fernando Valley.   Betty her husband in California through friends. Says Betty, "He was a Johnny Depp look alike and women everywhere threw themselves at him. He seldom failed to catch them!" They divorced after 13 years but remained friends until he died.

"I was always a ham and the movie industry attracted me," Betty recounts. San Fernando was close enough to give her easy access. She started out with a job decorating pottery.   She enrolled in acting classes and listed with an agent. Her personality and artistic talent served her well and she started getting jobs from central casting. Betty worked as an extra, did commercials, films and theater. She said her favorite thing was live theater. She sang, danced and acted in full costumes. Her theater group traveled all over the US and even Europe. "I was so excited when I got a call to go to Vienna. Austria was so different," said Betty. She also loved working in England. At home in the U.S., she also worked a lot of conventions. "When you go into that business you're a 'starving artist' and you just go from job to job," she smiles. After many years working in the field, her knees gave out and she couldn't dance anymore. That's when Betty decided she could not wake up one more day in the city. She needed space and nature.

Betty had attended the Mountain Festival in Tehachapi for years, and she decided this was where she wanted to live. She loved the mountains and the wilderness, and it was still close enough to go back and forth to the LA area. She said, "The people in Tehachapi were always so friendly and there was always somebody there if you needed help." So, sixteen years ago, she made Tehachapi her retirement home. Her horses retired with her. She loves the wild life of the area, and says there is a pack of coyotes that follows her around. She calls them yard dogs. "We live like pioneers and we get along with the wild life. We don't have lawns so we let the animals live their lives and they have become part of ours," she says.

Betty has more time now to give to her artwork, and her paintings of horses and wildlife can be found at the Treasure Trove in Tehachapi. Betty works in watercolor, acrylic and a little bit of oil but says her real love is clay. She may not dance professionally any more but her scintillating personality is still vivid and strong, and her artwork is a testimony to that strength and tenacity.

Life hasn't always been easy. Betty lost all three of her children at an early age. When asked what advice she would give others, Betty said, "Very few people live life without problems. I buried all my children. It wasn't easy. God gives you things to make you stronger. You just go with it. You just do your best. I really believe in a higher power. That higher power will not give you things to hurt you but to make you stronger. I was angry at God when I lost my son. I said I didn't believe anymore. My best friend said, 'Yes you do, because you couldn't be so angry with Him if you didn't believe.' Hold onto your faith and pray. Your higher power always gives you the strength to hang on."

CHECKING IN WITH YOURSELF

Sometimes our emotions are hidden from what we think is going on in our life. In this exercise you'll describe how you're truly feeling using images and words cut from a magazine.

1. Choose a picture from a magazine that describes your emotional mood. Glue it in your journal.
2. Cut out 5 or more words and create a collage around your chosen picture.
3. Meditate on your collage. Write any messages or thoughts in your journal and record whatever comes to mind.

CHAPTER 18 - LAURAINE SNELLING
AN EXTRAORDINARY GIFT

"There are painters who transform the sun to a yellow spot, but there are others who with the help of their art and their intelligence, transform a yellow spot into the sun" Pablo Picasso

One thing about Lauraine Snelling is that she is there for you. I always feel heard and acknowledged when I'm with Lauraine. Maybe it's because she is a writer, maybe it's because she loves the Lord. Whatever it is, her natural warmth and her caring heart always helps to make one feel comfortable.

A person who makes you feel safe has often been described as "someone who can hug the sadness out of you." Whether it's through her books, her watercolors, or just plain conversation, having Lauraine for a friend truly can "transform a yellow spot into the sun".

"Others have seen what is and asked why. I have seen what could be and asked why not. " Pablo Picasso

LAURAINE SNELLING

Lauraine Snelling was born in Chicago, Illinois, in 1942. Her mother was a nurse, and her father was overseas defending our country. Back then nurses were required to live at the hospital and you couldn't have children with you. Lauraine's mom hired a woman from social services to help out. "I lived with my Auntie Bobby, and my mom came to stay on her days off. When the war ended, I went on my first train ride to New York City where I met my dad for the first time, too. That was very normal for kids back then," said Lauraine

After the war, Lauraine's father went back to school in Bemidji, Minnesota and earned a degree in agriculture. The family bought a dairy farm and became farmers. Lauraine says she got her first pony when she was five. "My daddy put me on that little horse and slapped her on the rump and I fell off, screaming. Daddy picked me up and immediately put me back on my pony. His comment was, 'Just hang on!' That was my first life lesson--to just hang on. I've remembered it all through the years and I use that phrase whenever I do motivational speaking," said Lauraine.

Lauraine got her love of horses from her father. "I loved the draft horses because when the kids were around, they would check under their feet. There is that kind of mothering in horses," she recalls. "I treasure that part forever." She also remembers the train whistling at night, and learning to drive a tractor at seven. "We were doing old time farming," said Lauraine. "And now I write books about that life. I would ride my pony in spite of her stubborn resistance. Polly was in her 40's, and when she died one winter night, that was my first brush with death. Another life lesson learned on the farm."

But her favorite memory was learning to read. "I went to a brick school building where Mrs. Colebucket taught. She was also my father's teacher when he was young. The greatest gift you can give a child is to teach them to read," said Lauraine. To this day Lauraine not only loves to read, but she writes as well. Thank you to all the Mrs. Colebuckets of this world.

Lauraine went on to college where she met Wayne Snelling. Lauraine quit school to get married and have a family. They've been together now for 60 years. She and her husband started out as farmers, milking cows. Wayne eventually went into carpentry. They lived mostly in small towns, moving according to where the jobs took them.

They had three children, two boys and a girl. Kevin Lee Snelling, 56, lives and works in Beaverton, OR. Besides work, Kevin enjoys bass fishing, and has been in many tournaments. Marie Jeanice Snelling was an avid volley-ball player. Sadly, she went home to heaven before her twenty-first birthday, after suffering a second round of cancer. Brian Kenneth Snelling lives in Anderson Valley, CA, where he works in the wine industry, loves gardening, and his two Golden Retrievers, Asti and Enzo.

Lauraine was always interested in writing, but says it wasn't until God put his foot in the middle of her back and sent her to a writer's conference in Portland, Oregon that she truly began her literary career.

"There was so much there,"Lauraine says, "that when someone asked me what I wanted to write, I was totally overwhelmed. All I could say was that I wanted to write horse books for girls. One thing we were taught at the conference was to form a critique group and get together regularly. When I got home, three of us formed our group and met every week for five years. I've been writing ever since. My first published book, *The Race,* is a story of a girl and her thoroughbred race horse." Lauraine has published over 100 books. Most of them are still in print, and she continues to work with a literary agent. She also does motivational speaking. Lauraine says she likes to speak about the books she has written and the stories behind the stories.

They had been living in Vancouver, Washington, but in 1985 the family moved to California for Wayne's job. Lauraine didn't plan on staying. She wanted to move back to Vancouver, but says that God had different plans. At first they lived in the Castro Valley. Later, they moved to Martinez, where Lauraine worked in the retirement industry as a marketing and social director. Wayne became asthmatic when they lived in Martinez, and was forced to retire a few years later. In 1997, they moved to Tehachapi, seeking cleaner air for Wayne. They bought a house in which they still live, found a church home, and settled in.

Lauraine started watercolor painting and joined the art family at the Treasure Trove. She continues to paint and write, and has learned to love Tehachapi. She says there is something here that not only draws artistic people, but also draws art out of people.

Lauraine's advice to others is to first and foremost have the Lord as their savior. And she reminds us: "Don't give up. Just hang on, like my father always said."

FLOW PAINTING

I give credit for this lesson to www.shelleyklammer.com

Shelley is an expressive art therapist who provides workshops and online counseling.

Watercolor painting invites flow. When you feel stuck in an old pattern, you can sit with a palette of watercolors and let your emotions move and release.

1. Painful emotional experiences affect the heart. Rub your heart with circular motions and invite your heart to flow through your brush.
2. Invite the hurt energy inside your body to release onto your paper through the paint.
3. Meditate on your art and journal anything that comes to mind. Invite words and insights to arise from your body.

AFTERWORD

THE FORGOTTEN TALENT

Age has a privilege. Elderly men and women can afford to speak with a bluntness that young people seldom attempt. In working with my friends "the wisdom keepers" I often found that they gave more to me than I could ever give to them. By putting their experience into words, they taught me to feel again with an open heart and to see the world with new eyes. I learned to listen and to let go of expectations both of myself, and the world around me. In the next few pages I will share some of the stories I was told while I worked at a long-term care facility.

Everyone's story matters. In story-telling, we learn about life and about each other. *"When we haven't the time to listen to each others stories we seek out experts to tell us how to live."* Rachel Remen. I have found the wisdom keepers to be excellent experts.

I hope the stories of my friends will bless you as much as they have blessed me. They speak and I listen. We are both satisfied.

Satisfaction comes not from any outer achievement but from the richness of experiencing life and sharing the inner experience of life with others.
Dr. Rachel Remen, author, PhD

WILL YOU COME OUT AND PLAY?

I was sitting in the swing on the patio with Helen by my side. It was a beautiful, sunny day. We rocked back and forth listening to the birds as they fought over the seed the gardener had put in the bird feeder. Helen picked up a fallen feather and gave it to me. I picked her a flower. The bright colors of the spring flowers brought joy to my heart and a smile to my face. It felt so good just to take tie out. How seldom I allowed myself such a respite.

Helen took my hand and squeezed it gently as we watched other residents walking around the garden of the Alzheimer's unit. Helen's conversations do not always follow a coherent pattern, but if you listen closely, they always hold a precious gem.

Was it coincidence that day or could she read my mind? I do not know. Maybe she felt my vibrations and wanted to let me know in her own way the importance of doing things slowly and simply, a little at a time. Helen turned to me and said: "You can't go faster than a day. I have to do things the children are coming. You know these young people, they work so hard and worry so much. They run here and there to buy all these toys. They never have time to play with them." Then she squeezed my hand again and smiled.

What simple wisdom I thought. And if I hadn't taken my ten-minute break, I would have been too busy to hear the message. I have found her words to be so true. I began to take tie out to play checkers with my grandson, read a book, or see a movie. By slowing down and "playing" an unusual thing happened. I did not have to work so long and hard to survive. The change in my life from "hare" to "turtle" created financial abundance, less stress and new and wonderful opportunities to realize and express my creativity.

I went back the following week to share with Helen my newfound joy. She was no longer with us. Her parting touched my soul. The thought came to me so strongly: "Many things happen around you everyday which are telling you things about how to live better, but you have to be aware. It takes awareness." Just then a feather dropped out of nowhere and landed at my feet. I looked up at the sky and smiled. "Thank you Helen" I said.

DO YOU WANT TO KNOW WHAT'S WRONG?

We were all gathered in a circle for chair massages. Soft music was playing and the lights were dimmed as we gave hand massages to each of the residents. All of a sudden, Jason spoke up in a loud voice and said, "Would you please lower that music before it gives me a headache." And George replied, "Oh my God, Issak Perlman would be mortified if he found out his music gave someone a headache!" All of a sudden, our peaceful circle became a lively discussion group.

I quickly turned up the lights and joined the circle as wrong. No one is satisfied with the world they're in. that's why they're all so grouchy."

"That's right," said Jean. "and this is the first time I've ever been old so I'm going to enjoy every minute of it. Now please turn off that music."

"Well" said George. "When God said wait for kingdom come, it wasn't because he had a sense of humor. It was a commandment. I reckon you'll just have to wait a bit. It won't hurt any of us to have a little patience. Just slow down and listen to the music. You might even enjoy it. Waiting for kingdom come isn't hard if you remember to enjoy the precious moments. It's those little things that make life worth it."

I'M JUST LOOKING FOR SOMETHING

Cindy and I were sitting on the sofa in her apartment. I asked her to tell me about one of her favorite memories. She surprised me and said, "Well, did you know that by the time I was nine years old, I had been arrested five times."

"My gosh!" I said. "Where you a rebel?"

"Oh no!" she replied, "I was just looking for something. And besides I really loved the cookies and milk they gave me at the station while I waited for my parents to pick me up. You see, I used to wander off. I would just leave the house and go for a walk and then I would get lost. I remember one day sitting on a bench on the Brooklyn Bridge just staring out across the water. I was very curious. I was looking for something."

"Did you ever find what you were looking for Cindy?"

"Let's see. Did I ever find what I was looking for. Well, you know, people go through life too quickly and they don't really see what is going on. We can't really judge by appearances. We need to slow down and get to know people as they really are. Don't live life by what you hear, live life by experience. Take one day at a time. If the spirit ever asks you to do something, do it. If you don't, you will spend the rest of your life wondering what would have happened. Remember, don't do three or four things at once. Take one thing at a time. Go within and ask yourself what is my heart's desire?"

"Remember, no limitations. Where do I want to be? What do I want to be doing? When you begin to do what you truly want, the flow will open up again. So many times our perception of what others are thinking has nothing to do with the reality of their thoughts. So we put ourselves through martyrdom and hardship and then wonder why no one appreciates our sacrifices. This creates bitterness, resentment, and anger. The simple solution is to be true to ourselves first, then the joy within bubbles over and there is more than enough for everyone."

"You must watch yourself constantly to see what illuminates and ignites you. Then you will know what makes you sing and dance and laugh and love and then you will have found what you are looking for."

"Oh dear, I do ramble on so!"

Judith Campanaro

Judith Campanaro was born and raised in California. At an early age, she recognized art as her life path. An art therapist by trade, Judith holds a BA in Psychology, an MA in Professional Counseling and a Certificate of Advanced Graduate Studies in Art Therapy. From 1976-1986, Judith owned and operated The Hobbit School of Art in Ventura, California, where she taught both children and adults. In addition to teaching, Judith has had many solo shows both in the United States and the Caribbean. Her paintings are also included in numerous public and private Collections. Inspired by the work of Wassily Kandinsky, I strive to explore both cultural and personal expression. My goal is to provide through my personal work an unselfconscious language that helps one look a little closer at the world around us.
My Mission Statement is *To Facilitate Empowerment through Creative Expression*. My life is the expression of myself in my art. Painting and teaching are my passion. My current objective is to be true to who I really am as an artist, teacher and empowerment coach.

You can find out more about Judith and her art at:
http://www.judithcampanaro.com

"We don't stop playing because we grow old. We grow old because we stop playing."
George Bernard Shaw

"I have reached an age when, if someone tells me to wear socks, I don't have to."
Albert Einstein

"The longer I live, the more beautiful life becomes."
Frank Lloyd Wright

"Ageing is not lost youth but a new stage of opportunity and strength."
Betty Friedan

Made in the USA
San Bernardino, CA
03 September 2019